W9-ACA-448

To Sir Deacon

my best

Jim Simons

12-4-88

# Notes on Politics

# From Down the Road a Piece

by
Jim Kincaid

Foreword by
Bill Whitehurst

# Notes on Politics
## From Down the Road a Piece

## by Jim Kincaid

Edited by
Cathérine Kincaid

Illustrated by
Ragan Reaves

Book Design by
Jay Galloway

Elam Press

OTHER BOOKS BY JIM KINCAID

*Notes to My Friends*
*Notes from Elam*

# DEDICATION

This book is cheerfully and sincerely dedicated to the politicians of America. The wise ones who keep the ship of State afloat, the dedicated ones, wise or foolish, who keep it interesting, and the rest, who make it fun.

Especially to those who got together two hundred years ago and gave us a remarkable document called the Constitution whether they meant to, or not.

To the politicians, then and now and in between. Life is quite complicated with them, and because of them, but it would be so drab without them.

# FOREWORD

Whether or not the reader has read *Notes to My Friends* or *Notes from Elam,* or simply heard Jim Kincaid's evening commentaries on the WVEC-TV evening news, this work, *Notes on Politics,* deserves special attention. It somehow seems fitting that I should be given the opportunity to have the first word of comment on this book. After all, Jim had the last word on me and my political associates in the Congress for years. Since I was away in Washington during the week when many of his observations were made, I did not often hear them directly. But I did hear *about* them, because friends or constituents would often ask me with a chuckle if I had heard what Jim Kincaid had had to say about Congress that week. Having been on the receiving end of barbs and satires as a Member of Congress, I knew that I was fair game. Indeed, when I witnessed the antics of some of my colleagues, I was surprised when we weren't pierced by some of the satirical lances that were pointed our way.

But Jim Kincaid's wit has few sharp edges, even when he has a right to be outraged by the kind of unbelievable behavior that only Washington can generate. He has the rare gift of making his listener laugh and nod in agreement at the same time. And when he does strike a serious note it is never in a pretentious vein.

He is concerned without being condescending, a virtue not always found among some of the network commentators.

Since retiring from Congress I have been fortunate to be able to join the WVEC-TV family on a part-time basis. Leaving Washington was not difficult, but making friends with Jim Kincaid and everyone in the news department at WVEC-TV has made my homecoming a joy. One aspect of it that has been particularly gratifying has been to come to know Jim on a personal basis. He was warm in his welcome and has been helpful to me in my own limited contribution to the station. That easy-going manner that you see on your television screen is genuine. Off camera he manifests the same disarming humor and charm and I find myself naturally swapping political yarns and anecdotes with him. His own media stint in Washington provided him with a fund of them just as it did me in my eighteen years there.

It's this rich background combined with a keen human insight that has enabled Jim to produce consistently excellent commentaries night after night on Channel 13. That he has seen fit to publish these in his book will bring double pleasure to his countless viewers and admirers. Some may have missed a few of these "notes" when they were aired. Others will recall them and enjoy becoming reacquainted with them. For Jim Kincaid's "notes" are much like him—someone you like to visit with often. *Notes on Politics* will have that effect upon you. Jim Kincaid wears well.

Bill Whitehurst
Former Congressman
2nd District, Virginia

# INTRODUCTION

I read somewhere once a statement to the effect that politics is war without guns, and that war is politics with guns.

Seems to me that's a shabby way to talk about a grand old institution like war.

With war there is a tradition that it will be fought according to a set of rules. Of course, it rarely works out that way. But, there are rules and that is what distinguishes war from politics.

In politics, there are no rules. At least there are no written rules. That would spoil the fun. The rules of politics are all unwritten and that relieves the participants of any obligation to follow them.

In war, no self respecting general would ever refer to the head general on the other side as "my esteemed colleague." Generals may respect each other, but they never show it until the war is over, and no harm is done.

Politicians, on the other hand, refer to each other in deeply respectful terms, even while planning to hit each other in the most sensitive parts, their reputations, with blows that are base and unfair in the extreme.

A general, on the eve of battle, when asked his opinion of the general facing him in the field, will honestly tell you that he plans to go after the no good *blank blank* and hand him his *blank* on a platter.

The politician, in the same circumstances, on the eve of a hotly contested election will maintain that he feels that both he and his opponent have presented their views on the issues to the electorate, and, that reason will surely prevail and that the voters will speak to those issues by way of the ballot box, and, that he is sure in view of the strength of his own case and that the decision of the voters will be clearly in his favor.

What he means to say is, "I'll go after the no good *blank blank* and hand him his *blank* on a platter."

You'll notice that I used blanks to express ideas in the foregoing quotes. This was political.

You see, I am running for office, and when one is running for office, it is considered bad form to swear, or otherwise use profane language in public.

People admire such language from generals since they expect generals, engaged as they are in a violent sport, to use violent speech.

Politicians, on the other hand, are expected to do their violence in private, where it doesn't offend the ladies.

Politicians are allowed to do these things, of course — and, indeed, expected to do them — but to do them quietly and discreetly so that we, the voters, don't have to admit, even to ourselves, that we are aware of their human failings.

Americans are a funny race of people. We don't care what our politicians do as long as they give us an opportunity to believe that they didn't really do it.

· For example, in the early days of the current campaign we were presented with the possibility that one of the front runners in the campaign might possibly be a womanizer. That is to say, politely, that he might be the sort to step out on his wife if the opportunity presented itself.

That would not have bothered us a lot.

But, he presented a newspaper in Miami a golden opportunity to remove all doubt. We don't allow our politicians to do that. We require a certain amount of moral insulation from their venial sins.

The big sins we tolerate, whether they keep them from us or not.

Let's face it, the sexual conquests of the aforementioned presidential candidate may, or may not, have affected his qualities as a President of the United States. We'll never know. But, we have learned from history that some of our very best presidents have been adulterers and that their bedroom habits had little or nothing to do with their conduct of foreign policy.

But, when a sitting president in a recent election campaign handed a multi-million dollar contract to a shipyard that was neither equipped nor, as we learned later, qualified to do a major carrier repair job, and thus bought votes for his party with our, the taxpayers' money, not a single hint of scandal resulted.

Thieves we tolerate. Adulterers need not apply.

One of the greatest disappointments of my own presidential campaign is that not one newspaper, from Miami or anywhere else, has tried to catch me in an act of adultery. It makes me wonder if they consider me to be presidential material.

They should because I plan, when elected, to restore sanity to the conduct of the office of the presidency.

Politics has been described, by Hubert Humphrey I believe, as the art of the possible.

Most recent presidents, however, have tried to get along with Congress, which is clearly impossible.

I don't plan to try to get along with Congress at all. I will make Congress get along with me. And I won't let them go to dinner, or to bed, until they do.

Under English common law, bailiffs in a court were sworn to take a jury into a room where no conveniences of any kind were available, and to keep them there, without food or drink or sleep, until they arrived at a verdict in the case in question.

Bailiffs in American courts still take such an oath, but they don't take it seriously, of course.

Still, it seems to me to be a good model for a president to follow in dealing with Congress.

It will be my policy, when elected, to bring the Congress to an empty field on my farm at Elam and propose a program. They will then be left alone to debate that program, and act on it, and when they are finished, be allowed to go home to their spouses or whatever, it's none of my business.

The Constitution of the United States was written and approved under similar circumstances; and what's good enough for the founding fathers, it seems to me, should be good enough for latter day legislators.

It is my belief that air conditioning and restrooms have unconscionably slowed the legislative process.

The Congress will not be required to approve my programs, of course, merely to act on them and to give the people who hired them, the American voters, a full day's work for a full day's pay. We require that of plumbers, auto workers, and housewives. I see no reason why we shouldn't expect politicians who, after all, spend a great deal of their careers asking us for their jobs, to do those jobs.

Under my administration, deficit spending should become a thing of the past within months, if not sooner. I plan to eliminate congressional salaries altogether, and instead allow the members to split whatever surplus remains of the taxpayers' money after they have paid the nation's bills. I predict a surplus before the next house payment is due.

Of course, I may have some trouble with some of these programs, since some troublemaker is always bringing up the Constitution. But, the Constitution has never been taken too seriously by lawmakers in this country anyway. Most of them have never read it and precious few of those who have pay overmuch attention to it.

I should be able to get some programs through before anybody notices.

I won't be the first president to do that. How else can you explain the IRS?

When elected, I plan to appoint my personal financial adviser and accountant, Fast Frank, as head of the IRS, with a mandate to put it on a businesslike footing.

Keeping people so busy trying to figure out what the forms mean that they lose time from work, and thus don't make as much money on which to pay taxes, seems like bad business to me.

Fast Frank has already written a new, simplified Form 1040 that's easy to understand. It has only two lines. One asks how much money you got, the second reads to send it in.

Frank says it accomplishes the same thing as the current IRS rules but cuts out all the *blank*...er...paperwork. Frank's a good man with figures, but sometimes his grammar leaves something to be desired.

Frank believes we can put the country on a paying basis by employing some sound business principles.

He suggests, since Congress will be meeting at Elam, and we won't be using the Capitol building, that we can rent it out to somebody who can turn a profit.

According to Frank, the Rotunda would make a great skating rink, and the House and Senate chambers could be used to give Washington a decent burlesque theater.

I told him the American people would never permit obscenity right in the nation's Capitol. "Why not?", he asked, "they've never objected up till now!"

I have been accused of not taking American Government seriously. Wrong! I take American Government very seriously. It's politics that I don't take seriously. And that's not to say I don't take politicians seriously.

However much fun I may have at their expense, I wouldn't want you, gentle reader, to believe that I don't have the greatest respect and admiration for many, if not most, of the men and women who make this great constitutional democracy of ours work and, on the whole, work very well. But, when each of them has to worry about reapplying for his or her job every two or four or six years, and pleasing anything from thousands to millions of bosses, there is a likelihood that they will sometimes do things that are most likely to get them reelected. And, unfortunately, some of the things they do are not necessarily designed to benefit the body politic at large, so much as that arm or leg of the body that will be voting in the next election.

That's all right, too, to a degree, since the health of any particular part of the body has a direct bearing on how the body as a whole feels.

But, as uncomfortable as an ingrown toenail may be, we are unlikely to take that ingrown toenail to a brain surgeon.

I just have the uncomfortable feeling that we are, so to speak, often getting our toenails clipped at brain surgery prices and that ain't government, that's politics.

I could be wrong about that, of course, since I'm mixing medicine with government, and I don't have a degree in either one. But I feel that we need to diagnose some of our ills before we go hellbent for leather to treat them.

Among the ills I would like to see us work on up front would be an elimination of hypocrisy as a national legislative policy.

I share with many of my fellow Americans a sense of wonder at our ability to see great wrong in some actions, and a firm resolve to do something about those wrongs, and to have other, equally discernible wrongs perpetrated before our very eyes and pretend that they have never happened; or, if they did, that they were understandable and forgivable.

In the recent past, the Government of the United States ground to a virtual halt after it was learned that certain individuals working in the White House had attempted to ransom some American hostages held by terrorist factions in the Middle East by selling arms to Iran, and turning the profits from that sale to the benefit of anti-Communist forces in Central America.

Was it wrong? Of course it was.

Was it something new? Certainly not.

One of America's most revered recent chief executives personally approved and helped to engineer an attack on Cuba.

You may recall the Bay of Pigs.

You may recall also that the American-sponsored forces were overwhelmed within a matter of hours, many of them taken prisoner, and later offered for sale or, let's use the ugly word, ransom back to the United States.

Of course, Mister Castro didn't ask for arms, he had an ample supply of arms coming from the Soviet Union, he asked for tractors and got them; and there was no storm of indignation whatsoever. After all, you don't expect skulduggery in Camelot. Hell, it doesn't dare even rain in Camelot.

I think both these major mistakes came about as a result of politicians meddling in something they know nothing about. Namely, international politics.

American politicians are pretty good at domestic politics. But, when they get into the international arena, they are babes in the woods.

There is in international politics a very rigid and well

defined set of rules by which nations conduct business with one another. However, American politicians, especially in recent years, fail to notice that their counterparts in other countries, friends and adversaries alike, survive that set of rules by carefully paying them no serious attention whatever.

The most perplexing thing about American politicians to their opposite numbers overseas, is that they seem forever to be genuinely concerned about being fair, whether that turns out to be in America's national interest or not.

Such a state of mind would never occur to any successful western European politician. He would know full well that his constituents expect him to act in their interests, that is to say his nation's interests, whether that's fair or not.

Where they have us is that the American character demands fairness. We bend over backwards to be fair. We are the nation of the Marshall Plan. The nation that, instead of shipping home whatever was left of our defeated enemies' industrial capacity, as the Soviet Union did, did everything in its power to restore their capacity to compete with us. There are those who think we did too good a job of it. But, that's the way we are.

Of course, there have been sorry acts committed by Americans, in war and peace. We have produced our share of traitors and corrupt politicians, and perpetrators of atrocities, and, and... But you know the story. Never forget, though, that you know the story because our system allows it to be told. You know the story because our Constitution forbids the restraint of expression, no matter how shocking, or unpalatable, or humiliating. That is where our system differs so radically from others.

The British are a free people, of course, but that freedom is guaranteed, not by a constitution but by custom, and may be modified by the party in power, at will. Fortunately, the British people have been sensible enough, at least in modern times, never to put into power a party extreme enough to try. But, they could.

There are a number of constitutions here and there around the world that are the equal of the American Constitution in terms of guaranteeing the rights of citizens. Take the Soviet Constitution, for example. There is hardly a right or freedom expressed in the American Constitution that is not also in the Soviet document. In fact, the Soviet Union is now living under its fourth Constitution, and each one expands the people's rights—on paper.

Each Soviet citizen is guaranteed the right to have a free press, to be educated and housed, to express his views without fear. Discrimination in the Soviet Union on the basis of sex, race, or nationality is expressly forbidden. Any one of the member States of the Soviet Union is guaranteed the right to secede. And citizens, if they feel they've been wronged, may sue the State.

I could go on. The Soviet Constitution is a beautiful document, practically guaranteeing the citizen that he may not only pursue happiness, but be assured of catching it. Ours stops short of that. But, any discussion of the Soviet Constitution must include the one article that allows such a charter to be in force and yet allow the condition of human rights to remain in the sorry condition that prevails there. I quote "enjoyment by citizens of their rights and freedoms must not be to the detriment of the interests of the society or the State."

What a wonderful loophole. One that is subject to just one set of standards, and that set by the State, which is to say, the Communist party.

The major difference between the American and Soviet Constitutions is simply explained. Ours means what it says, even when it's uncomfortable.

But here I am getting all serious, and I don't want you to be scared off by that. This book isn't meant to persuade you to believe as I believe. Just to take a few glances at things and have some fun with them, or think about them, or cast them to the winds.

This book is a collection of thoughts I have had, in passing, as I've watched the world go by.

They are relatively short pieces, written as they were, for my daily television broadcast. Most of them may be read in two minutes or less. And, they do not need to be read in any paticular order.

You could well decide that some of them need not be read at all. That's up to you. You paid for it and it's your book.

Readers of my earlier books, *Notes To My Friends* and *Notes From Elam,* have noted that my books are particularly well suited for placement in the smallest but most essential room in the house. That is okay with me, I have done some of my most enjoyable reading there. Besides, there comes a time in anyone's life when he only needs to read for two minutes.

Incidentally, they're not all about politics; that was just a dodge to get you to buy the book.

Thanks, and I hope you enjoy it.

*The lobster tries to alert Jim that Murphy is about to make off with the chicken.*

Have you heard about this?

They're talking about selling off the federal government.

Not the whole government, of course, just parts of it.

The idea is based on the theory, some would call it a fact, that private enterprise can do just about anything government can do, and do it better, and not lose money on the deal.

In some States, as a matter of fact, private enterprise has taken over operation of the prisons, and it seems to be working.

There's a lot of talk in Washington about selling the federal housing system to private contractors and there's even been suggestions that the national park system could be run better by the rules of free enterprise.

I don't think they'll actually do it, you understand...

In Washington, on any given day, they're generally talking about doing something they never get around to doing—like spending only as much money as they take in, radical things like that.

But, in case you haven't noticed, the government is already operated, in large part, by private enterprise.

The way it works, the government decides that something has to be done about something, forms a department to handle that, and the department turns around and hires consultants to tell them how to do it.

Thus, we taxpayers pay the person the government hired to do something about something, and we also pay somebody else to tell him how to do it. When the sensible thing would be to hire somebody who knows how to do it in the first place...

I heard somebody describe a consultant as a guy who tells you what time it is—and uses your watch.

Nah, they won't sell the government—it makes too much sense.

*January 1986*

Since I mention our farm at Elam from time to time, the place where we Kincaids spend most of our weekends, folks sometimes walk up to me on the street or in a shopping center and ask:

Just where is Elam anyway?

A question I'm always happy to answer when I'm talking to somebody face to face and have a general idea what sort of person is asking the question.

I have generally located Elam on this broadcast in the past... It sits at the hub of the Pamplin-Prospect-Tuggle metropolitan complex.

But, in spite of all this, there are some people who don't believe there is any such place as Elam at all, and that I made the whole thing up.

Well, I want to put those rumors to rest.

There is indeed a community in Virginia named Elam. And it has a newspaper reporter.

It's not me. I do television and Elam doesn't have a television station, just yet, and it doesn't have a newspaper either; but the Farmville Herald carries dispatches from Elam written by Marge Swayne.

I've been trying to get Marge to do a series of articles on the crime wave we've had at Elam. After all, the highway sign has been stolen again. It's the sign up by Anderson Coleman's house. But the pressure of who's visiting whom for the holidays has kept Marge pretty busy on the society beat...

Besides, Anderson doesn't believe it's Elamites who have been stealing that sign, but people from Hampton Roads on vacation who never believed there was such a place as Elam, and who take the sign home with them to prove that there is; and they know where it is.

They just think they do...

With the sign gone I've missed Elam a couple of times myself.

*January 1986*

Folks, I have a serious philosophical problem here.

It's all because of this new bill before the Virginia Legislature that would require high school athletes to pass all their courses to be eligible to play on school teams.

Part of me thinks we should have such a law. After all, the purpose of an educational system is supposed to be education.

But, another part of me wonders what will happen under such a law to the student who has great athletic talent and little or no scholastic ability.

He loses, as a friend of mine pointed out this morning, the opportunity to do perhaps the only thing he or she is good at.

The arguments on both sides of the question are good.

I remember when I was in the Arkansas school system, many years ago, you had to have a C average to play school sports. But you also had to do that to be in the senior play, or to have the privilege of leaving school early for an after school job.

But, I also remember that some of our best athletes could squeeze onto the team with miserable grades in social studies and math because they invariably made A's in phys ed and shop. You don't have to know much math to build a bird house.

What's most troubling about the whole controversy is the fact that it's the same students who get hurt either way we go, either denied a chance to excel at something, or sent on with inadequate preparation for life after school days are over.

Maybe this is one of those problems that doesn't have an answer.

Or maybe, just maybe, we haven't looked hard enough—and in the right place—like somewhere around the first grade.

*January 1986*

I got to thinking about seed catalogs this afternoon. Some of you probably are already getting your seed catalogs in the mail, and enjoying the warm thoughts of spring and summer that they inspire.

I envy you.

I don't get many seed catalogs any more, and I think I know why.

I never buy anything out of seed catalogs.

I always intend to.

If I get a seed catalog in January or February, I always sit down the first chance I get and plan a garden.

I go through the seed catalog page by page, selecting the various crops that I fully intend to raise, some that I've raised in the past, and some new ones that I want to try this year.

*Every year, it's tomatoes.*

I circle all the pertinent items, and there are always a lot of them; then I total the prices of all the seeds and plants I plan to order, realize that the total comes to more than a grocery bill for a family of four for a year, and start editing...

By the time it's down to a reasonable figure I start watching the weather.

Finally, I realize it's too late to order seeds and still get them in the ground in time. So I wander into a hardware store and buy a few.

I'm a sucker for hardware stores. So I usually go over budget, and have to delay the remainder of my seed catalog order until my wife has forgotten what I spent on the trip to the hardware store.

Then I notice that everybody else already has a garden planted and decide I'll just raise a few tomatoes.

Back to the hardware store for a couple of plants already started which I put in the ground, every year, the night before the last frost.

*January 1986*

I was more than a little annoyed with some of my colleagues in the media today.

Within minutes of the disaster above Cape Canaveral, they were asking questions that could not, at least at that time, be answered.

Will this affect the American space program?

Of course it will. But how it will do that is impossible to say and will depend, of course, on the vision and the courage of those who have to carry on from here.

Seven lives were lost, seven good and productive and promising lives. And there will be an outcry, you can depend on it, that the cost of exploring space is much too high when we have to pay such a terrible price.

But it would compound today's tragedy, it would make those lost lives more tragic still if it causes us to decide that exploring and using space is not America's proper role.

Someone will do it, no matter what the cost.

Who that will be may depend in large part on how Americans react to today's demonstration—in terrible, shocking terms—of how dangerous human progress really is.

Our adversaries stave off the political effect of such disasters by merely ignoring the fact that they have happened. And they have, several times.

In our open and free society such secrecy is unavailable to comfort political leaders who have to make hard decisions—decisions that will most certainly cost lives.

Some will say, and have said already, that if the Almighty had intended humankind to fly, he would have given us wings.

Some will say he did, and we're still learning how to use them.

*January 1986*

When I was a youngster I didn't wear neckties unless I absolutely had to.

I think it was the association with events that made me dislike neckties.

About the only time I ever had to wear one was when there was a funeral, or a wedding, and at that time in my life I considered both these events to be tragedies.

Later, when I found the necktie necessary for jobs and social events in which I was interested, I usually acquired my neckties in the time honored way—I swiped them from my Dad.

Swiping ties from dads was not considered pre-criminal activity in my youth; just dangerous, if you happened to get one of his favorites.

Well, I've got a confession to make.

Since the only offspring at my house is a girl, I thought I was safe in the clothing category. After all, girls don't wear neckties, they swipe dresses from their mothers.

Wrong.

Girls these days will wear anything, as long as it's not something girls traditionally wear.

I haven't had a tee-shirt of my own in years.

Plaid flannel shirts, the kind that men wear hunting or on walks in the woods, teenage girls wear such things to parties.

I have to guard tweed jackets with a gun at my house.

If you don't have a teenaged daughter you can't appreciate this. But the only thing that will keep a teenager from stealing your clothes is if they, for some reason, fit.

No self-respecting teenager wears anything that fits these days.

Socks, long underwear, I'm telling you folks, nothing's safe these days. They'll wear anything.

Unless it looks respectable, of course.

*January 1986*

I've had several letters and phone calls lately complaining about the fact that I haven't mentioned Murphy, my Irish setter, lately and let folks know how he's doing.

Well, he's fine.

He hasn't reformed, or anything like that.

It's just that his recent outrages have been very similar to his previous crimes, and I thought you wouldn't be interested in hearing the same old story.

He has been singlehandedly responsible for the breakage of several more storm door window panels.

That's not meanness on Murphy's part, or anything like that, it's just that Murphy often finds himself on the other side of a storm door from where he prefers to be; and he seems to consider a closed storm door a mere inconvenience.

I've considered installing a storm door that Murphy can't jump through when it's closed, but my contacts in the storm door trade say they don't make 'em out of armor plate.

We have a white board fence around the yard at Elam now that Murphy can jump over, but he doesn't know he can since he has dug several exits under the fence.

It does, however, slow him down enough that pickup trucks driving by are relatively safe.

Tractors, on the other hand, still pass the house at Elam at their own risk.

We built the fence at Elam specifically to keep Murphy from chasing the neighbors.

It worked, for most of one afternoon.

But aside from breaking through storm doors, defeating expensive white board fences, sleeping on couches that we don't want him to sleep on, and stealing anything that even resembles food, Murphy is quite well behaved.

I guess he's getting old.

*January 1986*

There's been a great deal of talk about the new policy of openness being practised in the Soviet Union.

After seventy years, the leaders of the Communist Party seem to be willing to talk about things they've never talked about before.

For instance. A few days ago, fifty or so former Soviet

citizens who had fled to the West for one reason or another in the past, went home to the Soviet Union, and were welcomed with open arms. And the Western press was invited to see the joyous homecoming which was, after all, clear proof that the freedom of the West was not at all it was cracked up to be.

Of course, they didn't point out—nor would any reasonable person expect them to—that hundreds of thousands of people have fled the workers' paradise in recent years and that when fifty decide that was the wrong decision it doesn't prove our system a failure at all.

Then there's Afghanistan.

The Soviet leaders have finally started admitting to their own people that there is a war in Afghanistan, and that Soviet soldiers are fighting in it and—that they'd just love to pull out if only the United States would stop supporting the rebels...

Of course, they don't mention that there was nothing to rebel against until the Soviet Union installed a government that went against the grain of the beliefs of the Afghan people.

Glasnost they call it—openness—and it's a wonderful thing if we don't get lulled into confusing it with the sort of truth that bubbles to the surface in a truly open society.

Abe Lincoln is credited with saying: "You can fool all of the people some of the time and some of the people all of the time, but you can't fool all of the people all of the time."

The trouble I have with the Soviet system is that, if you control all of the people all of the time it doesn't really matter all that much whether you can fool them or not.

So, that remains—as it has since 1917—the number one item on the Soviet agenda.

*January 1987*

In case you haven't heard, there's more than one scandal cooking in Washington these days.

Of course, there's the Iran Contra affair, with the president right in the middle, and what did he know and when did he know, and—as one wag put it—if he knew, did he know that he knew syndrome.

You know about as much about that one as I do, and probably as much as Sam Donaldson or the Senate Foreign Relations Committee knows.

But, the other scandal may have escaped your notice.

You see, it snowed in Washington last week, about the same time it snowed in Virginia, but more of it.

Well, the streets of Washington didn't get plowed very thoroughly, and while a lot of Washingtonians were suffering clogged streets and stranded cars, Mayor Marion Barry was in California, attending the Super Bowl.

To make matters worse, the Metro system broke down, and between the snow, clogged streets, a subway that wouldn't work and the mayor off in California enjoying himself, the citizenry of our nation's capital is up in arms.

At least, the Washington Post says it is, and has called for the convening of a panel of experts to study the situation.

Only in Washington.

While all this was going on, the City of Washington found time to serve a warrant on a fellow who owns a bulldozer and had it at home and took it upon himself to plow his street and several neighboring streets.

You just can't have people stepping in and doing the job government is supposed to do, even if government doesn't do it.

A lot of what goes on in Washington mystifies me. But I do know one thing about officialdom there—they have a marvelous talent for missing the point.

*January 1986*

I heard a statement a few days ago that really distressed me.

It was on one of those Sunday talk shows that all three networks have, where journalists talk to the movers and shakers in Washington.

On this particular occasion I heard a senator, a man whose name you'd immediately recognize, say that there must be a tax increase, and that it will have to be this year, because the following year is an election year.

Now, I realize that politicians behave differently in election years than they do in non-election years; but I hardly expected to hear one admit it in no uncertain terms on national television.

Folks, they really do believe that we—the voters—will forget what they do to us in non-election years in the welter of promises they plan to make to us in election years.

And they're right.

I don't know whether we need a tax increase or not just now. I do know that I don't feel a personal need for a tax increase. But, I stand ready to be convinced that we have to pay for what we get, and we haven't been doing that.

I'm not totally convinced that we need all we've been getting, or that if we give the Congress enough of our money to pay for it, that they won't cast about and find some other things we don't need to spend it on—like projects that will help them get reelected.

They do that you know.

Mark Twain once pointed out that a cat who sits on a hot stove lid will never sit on a hot stove lid again. It draws a lesson from the experience and remembers it in all future encounters with hot stove lids, even in an election year.

Which would indicate that cats are somewhat superior to American voters who get burned repeatedly but don't seem to be able to remember once they get near a voting booth.

*January 1987*

It was terribly tempting to arrange to be snowbound at Elam today.

And I probably could have gotten away with it.

After all, there was already a foot of snow on the ground out there in Prince Edward County, and what with that that started falling yesterday, the total accumulation is now about twice that.

Yessir, I could have called in this morning and told the boss that I was up to my eyeballs in snow and he would have believed me.

I knew that when I started for Norfolk early yesterday, but I came anyway...

For one thing, my wife was here, having stayed in town for the weekend to catch up on some family bookkeeping.

When there's going to be a snowstorm I always like to be on the same side of it that my wife is on.

For another, Murphy and the other dogs of Elam spend a lot of time indoors by the fire when the weather's like this. And, it gets a tad aromatic around the fireplace.

It's not that my five dogs are unclean, or anything like that, but they're generally outdoor dogs—and shaggy outdoor dogs at that—and after a run in the woods, with deep snow getting into their hair and then bringing them in to warm up by the fire, well—it's no place for anybody with a sense of smell.

I mean, inside like that you can't get upwind of them.

I had to break for air several times and when I did, the dogs broke with me, picking up a new layer of snow to thaw out each time.

I asked my father-in-law how he could stand it. And he said, after a while it closes your sinuses so thoroughly you can't smell anything.

That's when an overwhelming sense of duty hit me and I headed east.

*January 1987*

I hardly ever read the sports pages, but I do try to pay attention when Roger Cawthon reports because it's exciting.

Sometimes Roger sounds excited about something that I wouldn't ordinarily get excited over, but then, I'm not your typical sports fan.

I do, however, get pretty interested along about this time of year about the Super Bowl.

For one thing, we almost always have a power failure at Elam on Super Bowl Sunday.

I don't necessarily believe that the Super Bowl has anything to do with the power failure, but the weather long about this time of year is usually anything but clement. And the power has a tendency to fail at Elam when the weather is even slightly less than clement.

Power failures on days other than Super Bowl Sundays are just an inconvenience, but on Super Bowl Sundays they are a major problem.

My father-in-law, you see, loves football and hates Jimmy the Greek.

All season long he follows the fortunes of all the professional teams, watches every game, knows the statistics, and chooses his favorites by a very democratic method. Which is to say, he always bets against the team Jimmy the Greek believes will win.

He just can't stand Jimmy the Greek.

If the officials make a bad call, he believes Jimmy

the Greek had something to do with it.

I don't know who he's for in the Super Bowl, I sorta like Chicago myself, but I'll know soon enough—when Jimmy the Greek makes his prediction.

Theo figures Jimmy the Greek won't have a power failure and will therefore be able to influence his pick to victory. While, if the power is off, Theo's favorite will have to flounder along without him.

And you thought it was just between the Patriots and the Bears.

*January 1987*

Good weather is always welcome long about this time of year.

We need something to convince us that winter is not a permanent condition, that the sun will shine again, and that it is possible for a human being to survive in the out-of-doors without several pounds of protective clothing.

We had such a weekend at Elam.

Imagine, seventy plus degrees and the grass didn't even need cutting. How could you ask for more?

But good weather is a mixed blessing at Elam since the heating bill goes down, but the food bill goes up.

The way that works—the kitchen door at Elam usually is opened more often when the weather is warm, and often is allowed to stay open for long periods of time; which is okay as long as there is someone present in the kitchen, or all the food is locked away.

Murphy, our senior Irish setter, is also Elam's senior food thief and he practices his art at every opportunity.

His favorite method is to spot something edible, any-thing edible, on a table or counter; and then manufac-ture an air of complete indifference to that item.

This weekend he ignored a large batch of dinner rolls, then bided his time until, of the four or five hu-mans then present in the vicinity, not one was specifi-cally watching those dinner rolls.

There came such a ten or fifteen second period, and needless to say, the dinner rolls were history and the rest of us made do with sliced bread, humbly grate-ful that the roast was in the oven at the time.

Then, later in the woods, he has the gall to come around wanting some of my chocolate chip cookies that I snuck out of the kitchen myself.

That dog's got no conscience.

*February 1985*

In the more than six years I've been relating my thoughts and experiences on this program, the viewers have been unfailingly helpful, and from time to time I feel I should pass along some of the good advice I get.

For example, Jean Walston of Elizabeth City heard me complaining a few days ago about my cold and the fact that I didn't deserve it since I had obeyed my wife in every way; I had dressed warmly, taken plenty of vitamins, especially Vitamin C, and had eaten all my broccoli.

Well, Jean says the cause of the cold had nothing to do with what you eat.

Doorknobs are the problem.

They collect the various viruses which cause colds from people with colds and save them for people with-out colds.

Just avoid doorknobs, Jean says, and you can skip the broccoli.

Jean says it's also safe to kiss your wife if you or she has a cold. But don't shake hands with her, and don't use the same doorknob.

Jean didn't say where the information came from. But I figure anybody who finds broccoli to be unnecessary to the continuance of life as we know it, is clearly thinking straight, and should be listened to.

Broccoli is something we will probably have to endure as long as there are wives and mothers in this world. And I guess that goes for colds as well—as long as there are doorknobs.

*February 1985*

I mentioned last week that I have been asked to run for president.

Some folks in North Carolina say they'll support me if I will run and that I need only say the word and they'll begin the campaign.

Well, I said then, and I'll say again, that I have no plans, at present, to run for president. And that's final, for the moment...

I have discussed it at length with my campaign manager and my fund raising committee, and they agree, a Kincaid for President Movement has little chance of success in the current political climate.

That means we don't have the money.

Politicians have to talk like that.

For example, Senator Lloyd Bentsen of Texas, the new chairman of the Senate Finance Committee has decided that it might be nice to have breakfast once a month with a group of lobbyists.

He wants to exchange meaningful dialogue with them on matters that might come before the committee such as laws that might benefit their clients.

He didn't say that last line, I did, but you can take it to the bank.

Another thing he wants to exchange with them is checks, for ten thousand dollars, which will go into his reelection campaign for the 1988 election, in which he does not yet have an opponent. But he's pretty sure he'll have one and a tough one at that.

Of course, those political action committees and special interest lobbyists don't expect their ten grand breakfasts with Senator Bentsen to sway his influence on legislation...

I guess the reason I don't want to mount a national political campaign just now is that such an interpretation of integrity is just too hard to bring off—with a straight face.

*February 1987*

When it comes to pure entertainment value, I don't think anything can beat a legislative body...

Especially the United States Congress.

Now, before I go any further I'd just like to say that I believe the vast majority of the men and women in the House of Representatives and the Senate of the United States are good and decent people. And they deserve to be paid more than they're currently getting.

Especially the ones from Virginia.

Just about every one of them could be making more money doing something else.

And it's our good fortune that they're not doing something else.

They're representing and senating for us in one of the world's most expensive cities and not a one of them makes as much as a shortstop on a last place major league baseball team.

But, and this is the fun part, they're about to get a raise.

That's right. Unless they do something to head off the twelve-thousand-dollar raise that's written into the law at the moment, they're going to get a raise at midnight tonight.

That's not the problem. The City of Washington can separate the most frugal legislator from twelve extra thousand dollars in no time at all.

No, the problem is that they have to take this raise while giving the outward appearance of being foursquare against it.

I haven't seen such high drama since Brer Rabbit begged not to be tossed into the briar patch.

The Senate has already gone on record as not wanting the pay raise. And you won't find anybody in the House who'll say anything nice about a pay raise this close to an election year; but with almost universal disapproval, that pay raise will nearly certainly be in the next checks.

*February 1987*

I guess I'm going to have to reverse my field and run for president after all.

Since I mentioned some days ago that a group in North Carolina has asked me to run, there has been a groundswell of public opinion urging me to do just that.

In fact, at least three people have written or called in and said that they will support me, as long as I don't ask for money.

Well, money won't be a problem. I plan to finance my campaign with my tax refund, if any. And if I need more, I'll just call up Oral Roberts and see how to go about making special financial arrangements with the Almighty.

It won't be necessary to attend either of the major party political conventions and seek a nomination.

If you get such a nomination, they start doing public opinion polls about you, and you have to go places like Iowa, and New Hampshire, and make all sorts of ridiculous promises. And do it in cold weather at that. And before you know it, Sam Donaldson is at your elbow wanting to know what you meant by what you said at the last campaign stop. And when you tell him to shove off, he just yells the questions at you from a distance.

Well, maybe I exaggerate. Sam is a really nice guy. And pretty polite, unless you happen to get elected.

But I digress.

I plan to conduct my campaign for the White House from the front porch of the old house at Elam, from two to four on alternate Sunday afternoons.

I plan to ask Jeane Kirkpatrick to be my vice president, and if we're elected, put her in charge of evicting the United Nations and renting the building out to tenants who will pay their rent and act in a civil manner.

Aside from that I don't plan any major changes in national policy, yet.

I'll keep you posted.

*February 1987*


Today (2/12/87) being President Abraham Lincoln's birthday — his real birthday — whatever the Congress may decide now or in the future, I thought it might be nice to look up some of the things he said and stood for that might be applied to things that are going on today.

Time, as the philosopher said, is a great healer. And by the time you and I came along and were encouraged by our teachers to learn about history, we probably learned only that Lincoln was a great man who freed the slaves and saved the Union.

You hardly ever hear anybody say anything bad about Lincoln these days.

But, at the time, there were newspapers that considered saying bad things about Lincoln to be their sacred duty. And, if there had been television in those days, there would probably have been television networks with the same sense of duty.

In fact, if there had been television in those days, it's highly doubtful that Lincoln would have been elected in the first place.

He didn't look presidential.

He wasn't particularly handsome.

He had, from all reports, a squeaky voice.

But, if he were around today and president, he might repeat a conversation he had with a fellow named Carpenter.

He said, "if the end brings me out all right, what is being said about me won't amount to anything. If the end brings me out wrong, ten angels swearing I was right won't make any difference."

It's probably good that we didn't have television then.

It makes a fellow wonder if we shouldn't have a law requiring our presidents to stay out of sight of television cameras for the time they're in office.

They might, in that case, get some useful work done. And history would judge them anyway, but at a more convenient time.

*February 1987*

Well folks, it looks like I opened a Pandora's box when I announced my candidacy for president.

The switchboard here at WVEC was deluged with two

*Jim opens a Pandora's box.*

or three calls within a mere matter of hours.

One was from a fellow who wanted to know about my campaign platform. And I told him I didn't think I needed one, I'll just use the front porch of the house at Elam. And he said no, he didn't think I quite understood, he wanted to know what principles I planned to run on. And I said "high principles," what else?

Which ones, he said; and I said, all of them, naturally.

Another caller wanted to know if I was looking forward to living in the White House. And I said no. I don't plan to live there at all. I plan, when I'm elected, to move the federal government to my farm at Elam.

I've got an empty pasture that the Congress can meet in and we can set up some tents in case it rains. And once they've balanced the budget, I'll let them go home and sleep in their own beds. There's no place to park their cars in Washington anyway.

I figure with Mario Cuomo and Gary Hart waiting for the Democrat party to make up its mind, and George Bush and Jesse Helms waiting for the Republican Convention, and Pat Robertson waiting for the nod from the Republicans (and the Almighty), that sorta makes me the front runner right now. Those other guys are waiting for somebody to nominate them, I'm running.

One of my detractors has charged already that I am politically naive, totally inexperienced in government, fiscally irresponsible, lacking in basic understanding of constitutional principles, and demanded a response to these charges.

That's easy—you can't please everybody.

*February 1987*

So the first episode of Amerika (with a "k") has, as the sportscasters would say, gone into the record books and the Republic still stands.

I suspect it will survive, at least until next Sunday, and maybe even beyond.

Frankly folks, I find this whole debate about whether "Amerika" is a good thing, or a bad thing, rather amusing.

We took a rather well deserved beating about the head and shoulders last night after our late news broadcast for only hearing out one side of the story, that is, the liberal opinion that the showing of such a program on American television can only increase the strain and mistrust between this country and the Soviet Union.

If it's any help, I hold the other view, that it is a good thing for Americans to be caused to think about what life might be like if we ever bargain away our freedom for mere safety.

As for "Amerika" diminishing the trust that I have in the Soviet leaders — no program could do that. I watched the first episode of Amerika last night and noticed that the writer had portrayed a fictional Amerika under Soviet domination that was not at all unlike some non-fictional countries I have seen, with my own eyes.

But I doubt that any fiction we, who are free, can read or watch on television can adequately describe the reality of a Hungary in the fifties, a Czechoslovakia in the sixties, the last few years in Afghanistan, or for that matter, Moscow last week where the new "openness" was put to the lie in the streets when people tried to demonstrate in favor of a prisoner of conscience.

If Amerika provokes us to think, I consider that a good thing. But you and I may differ on that.

Isn't it nice that neither of us can send the other to jail for holding a wrong opinion?

*February 1987*


I guess the course of politics, like that of true love, never runs smooth.

Here I was, all ready to finance my campaign for the presidency with whatever money my accountant, Fast Frank, can get back from the IRS and then...Zounds—that's a word you can use when you can't use the word you really want to use—Zounds, nature intervenes.

It appears my political career may have to give way to the plumbing industry.

Last night, after staving off cold spells all winter, the old farmhouse at Elam admitted enough of winter's icy blast to freeze the water pipes.

And naturally, to freeze them at a spot where they've never frozen before.

Folks, over the past ten years I have completely replaced the plumbing system at Elam, one foot at a time.

Well, I got the news this morning from my father-in-law who lives at Elam year round, and claims to like it there, that there is a spot in the plumbing system that burst last night that should provide area plumbers with a new challenge.

I don't know exactly where it is, but I do know from past experience, that it will require major structural dismantling to get there; and that it will take highly skilled specialists in the trade many extrordinarily expensive hours to get there.

And if that's not bad enough, they'll have to get to the house itself through about fifteen inches of so far unplowed snow.

Past experience also tells me that these guys start their clocks the minute weather conditions indicate a plumbing problem at Elam, then go back to bed and wait for my call, secure in the knowledge that tuition for their kids isn't going to be a problem this year.

I'm not sure any presidential campaign can stand such a blow. But if I survive—and win—the deficit should be no problem.

*February 1987*

Much of the mail this week had to do with my campaign for the presidency, which is, I'm happy to report, back on track.

Mary Haas, in fact, had a dream that I had been elected and after my first state of the Union address, which was three minutes long and sandwiched between the local and national news, that Sam Donaldson and George Will agreed with everything I said.

Mary did wonder if it would really be such a good idea for me to be president since in Washington my dog Murphy would have nothing to chase, except maybe lawyers and lobbyists.

Don McAdams stated flatly that he would not support me for president. But that he would consider a ticket that included my Irish setter Murphy or Joe Foulkes's dalmation, Ahab.

Sorry Don, but Murphy and Ahab have already been picked to head up my Bureau of Management and Budget.

A nitpicker here at the office said that's ridiculous, that dogs don't know anything about managing money.

I said, since when is that a qualification?

I was especially pleased with the letter from the Reverend Ron Davidson, formerly of Oxford Furnace, Virginia, who wants to run as my vice presidential running mate.

He believes that the two of us, with our rural backgrounds, can teach Congress a thing or two about the proper and efficient use of horse manure.

The Reverend Ron also believes he, being a minister, may be able to carry some of the vote that might otherwise go to Pat Robertson.

Says his children will vote for us, but he's not sure about his wife and the family cat.

Sounds like a solid ticket to me, Ron. And I am considering it.

I figure, if we could divert a hurricane right close to the election that could sew it up for us.

Anyway, thanks for writing friends and neighbors, and keep those letters and cards coming in.

*February 1987*

Imagine my pleasure when I got a letter from my running mate in my campaign for the presidency.

Ron Davidson, whose membership in the clergy we hope will overcome the Pat Robertson factor, got to be my running mate by being the first to ask.

The fact that he's the only one who asked is just coincidental.

Anyway, Ron had some excellent ideas on a cabinet made up of country folk, and I was especially taken with his thoughts on a Secretary of Defense.

He'd choose a former prisoner of war who would have a particularly sound grasp of the nature of our adversaries and the loss of freedom.

Good idea.

Mrs. H.R.T. of Elizabeth City recalled a tour she once made in Europe and a trip to East Germany where, at one stop, the tourists were forbidden to take pictures.

It was at a Russian restaurant.

Well, I've eaten at Russian restaurants, in Russia, and I can't say I really blame them for wanting to keep them secret.

The only thing worse than the food was the service.

Henry, Liz, and Myrt think running the government at Elam is a good idea. And Stanley Bachmurski, who describes himself as a country boy, wants to be Secretary of State.

I'll have to get Stanley and Vice President Reverend Ron together. But he certainly seems qualified.

B.L. "Kinky" Berry thinks I am probably not qualified for the presidency. Says I couldn't tell a lie if I had to.

Sure I could. Elect me.

Actually, that's no problem. Even if I couldn't lie I'd be able to pick it up within minutes in Washington, with so much expert help around.

George Washington, incidentally, never claimed to be unable to tell a lie. That story was fabricated by a minister named Parson Weems who probably should have gone into government himself.

Thanks for writing friends and neighbors, and keep those cards and letters coming in.

*February 1987*

Most of us learned sometime in high school that Julius Caesar was murdered on the Ides of March.

Most of us don't remember what year it was, but we do know that it was on the Ides of March of that year, whenever it was.

But, do any of us know, or did we ever know, what an Ide is?

I certainly didn't. Not until today, and I'm not sure I know even after the extensive and painstaking research I did this afternoon.

Some of the younger members of the studio crew, the ones you never see, but who are a hard working and diligent lot, asked me in passing if I knew what an Ide is, and I had to admit that I didn't.

So, I set out to learn about Ides. And this is what I found out.

The Romans felt strongly about their months and where they happened to be in any given month. So they identified the middle of several of them as the Ides; not all of them, just some of them like March, May, July, and October.

The Ides of the other months come on the thirteenth. I don't know why, they just do.

So, we know generally just when Ides happen, but in all the references there was nothing to describe what an Ide is, or why anybody would need one in the first place.

I believe I'm safe in saying that Ides only come in pairs or sets, since there's no record of an Ide happening by itself.

But it wasn't a total waste of time since I learned something else about Caesar's Ides of March.

It seems there were sixty conspirators who wanted to end Caesar's dictatorship and restore democracy and did that by stabbing him twenty-three times.

A dubious beginning, since clearly thirty-seven of them didn't get a turn.

*March 1985*

The swallows came back to Capistrano today.

They always do.

They come back so faithfully that tourists and townspeople gather at the Mission of San Juan Capistrano in California each year on this day and if the swallows have ever failed to arrive on time, they've kept quiet about it.

About a half dozen showed up today.

Nobody ever said that all the swallows come back on time.

Of course, that's over three thousand miles from here, but the return of the swallows always gives me a lift.

It goes along with all the other events of the season that celebrate the fact that the weather will be warmer in the months to come and the days will have more daylight in them for us to enjoy the warmer weather.

The vernal equinox is tomorrow at eleven fourteen in the morning and the daylight hours and the darkness hours will be approximately the same duration. But that's all too scientific for my taste.

Give me swallows at Capistrano and the jonquils my wife and I found in the woods of Elam last weekend.

There once was a house where we found those jonquils. The jonquils and a pile of old handmade bricks all tangled up with honeysuckle vines and a tiny graveyard with two ancient headstones tell us a rather nice story.

That man and his wife loved that land enough to want to stay for good. The headstones say so.

They warmed themselves by a fireplace in the winter, the bricks tell us that.

And I suspect they had an almanac that would tell them when the vernal equinox would take place. And jonquils to confirm it.

*March 1985*


I was somewhat disappointed last Sunday afternoon when I made a campaign speech in my bid for the presidency from the front porch at Elam.

There was nobody there.

And it was a good speech.

I made some really fantastic promises and perhaps it's just as well that nobody showed up, because there's always some busybody that insists on remembering campaign promises after an election.

*Swallows show the beginning and end of summer.*

In fact, it happened to Governor Baliles not long ago.

Some grouch remembered, right after he got the Virginia Legislature to raise taxes, that he had indicated back during the campaign that he was against higher taxes.

Ronald Reagan and Jimmy Carter both promised to decrease the size of government, then got elected and increased the size of government.

It's some sort of political law: You've gotta break your promises or there's no sport in it.

Well, my supporters can rest easy. I intend to keep all the promises that I get caught at.

Some will have built-in deniability, which is a Washington word for "I never said that and if I did I probably meant something else; I don't remember exactly."

As you can see, my grasp of the language of Washington politics is unimpeachable.

Another thing I missed Sunday during my campaign appearance was a gaggle of Washington reporters shouting questions at me.

My dogs did bark a few times though and I pretended it was reporters shouting questions, just for the practice.

I believe, in retrospect, that the cause of good government was well served in terms of the vital information developed during the whole exercise.

Throw them something and they'll leave you alone. I used dog biscuits. President Reagan might try North and Poindexter.

*March 1987*


Much has been made in the press and in the broadcast media these past few days about the verbal scuffle that's going on among some of the TV preachers.

This latest round started with the revelation that PTL

Evangelist Jim Bakker misbehaved some years ago—and admits it—but blames it on treachery by former friends and says recent rumors about the matter were spread by another evangelist intent on taking over his ministry.

Now, another evangelist, Jimmy Swaggart, says he didn't spread the rumors about Bakker, but believes they're true, and that he doesn't want the PTL ministry.

Oral Roberts, out in Tulsa, took time out from dealing with a death threat from the Almighty and a wrestling match with the devil to weigh in with the opinion that Swaggart is taking a holier than thou attitude in this whole mess, and should be ashamed of himself.

And ... and ... well, folks ... it gets complicateder and seamier the deeper you delve into it.

I've heard it described as either a civil war, or a holy war, and I don't think it's either civil—or holy.

It's something else.

But, I'd just like to toss in the thought that we must be very careful here not to throw out the baby with the bathwater.

There's nothing wrong with evangelism, and there's nothing wrong with doing it on television.

I believe if the apostles had had television they would have used it, and they would have used it to spread the word and garner help for the needy.

And, if mankind were perfect, Moses wouldn't have had to make two trips up the mountain to pick up a full set of commandments.

If I read the Bible right, that too was a case of putting entertainment values ahead of theology.

*March 1987*

A fellow walked up to me at a dinner meeting a few nights ago and asked if he could ask me a question.

That always makes me nervous when people ask if they can ask me a question.

It usually means that the question they're going to ask is one that you either would rather they didn't ask because you don't know the answer, or, one that you'd rather they didn't ask because you do know the answer.

But, when somebody asks if you mind if they ask you a question you have to lie and say you don't mind. Because if you say yes, you do mind if they ask you a question, that sounds like you already know that the question they plan to ask is one that you'd rather they don't ask.

You see the problem.

Anyway, this fellow asked if I minded if he asked me a question, and I lied and said I didn't, and he asked me why it is that the networks believe that those of us out here in television land are interested in every little detail even remotely connected to the Iran arms affair, and that they have to tell us the minute they learn something.

I said I didn't know, that that bothers me too.

He said he was watching programs several times last week and several times Tom, or Dan or Peter broke in and told him things at four o'clock or so in the afternoon that he could have waited till six or six thirty to find out. And that on each occasion they messed up the program he was watching. He mentioned particularly one of those courtroom shows. And said he heard most of the evidence, but never heard the verdict, and that he'd much rather they wouldn't do that unless it was something like a hurricane or an incoming nuclear rocket, or something.

I told him I felt the same way, and did that answer his question.

He said, sorta, and I said that's closer than I expected.

*March 1987*

A poll published in the New York Times concerning the scandal involving television Evangelist Jim Bakker indicates that at least somebody has benefited from the whole seamy affair.

Namely—the devil.

Yessir, the Times polled over five hundred viewers of evangelical television and discovered, with a margin of error of plus or minus four points, that for everybody who believes the devil was responsible in this matter, there is an equal number who believe he was innocent.

Or, maybe if not innocent just uninvolved.

According to the Times, forty-three percent believe the devil was responsible and forty-three percent think he was not responsible.

That, I believe, is a considerable improvement in the devil's popularity rating since I was a youngster.

We used to believe that the devil was responsible for all the evil in the world.

But those were more conservative times, I guess.

Now, personally, I believe the devil was behind this mess somewhere, no matter what the New York Times poll says. But I will admit to being less certain of his guilt than I was before the poll.

Maybe Mark Twain was right.

He said the devil never really got a fair shake. That everybody, including all the preachers, talked about him, but nobody ever told his side of the story.

Twain went on to say that he had a certain grudging admiration for the devil's accomplishments which had enabled him to become the spiritual leader of four fifths of mankind, and the political leader of all of it.

I think Mark Twain may have stretched things there a bit but I'm in no position to judge.

I embellish a bit myself from time to time.

Course, it's not my fault, the devil makes me do it.

*March 1987*

*Never put a hammock in your wife's view.*
*(Also make sure it's higher than your dog.)*

This is my favorite season of all for spending weekends on the farm at Elam.

There's nothing that needs cutting right now.

For most of the year either it's necessary to spend time cutting wood to keep from freezing to death or it's necessary to cut grass so I can find the driveway.

But every year, for a blessed few days, the cutting tools can lie idle.

We have enough wood on hand, I believe, to last until the chimney sweeps move back in.

We always know when it's time to stop building fires at Elam by the whirring in the chimneys.

Then, in the fall, when the chimney sweeps leave, we know it's time to check the woodpile and see if there's enough there to get through the cold months.

There never is.

So, we stop cutting grass and start cutting wood.

But this weekend I expect to have enough idle time to be able to do my annual research on where to hang my hammock.

Hammock hanging can't be taken too lightly, placement is everything.

Hammocks should always be hung out of the direct line of vision from a kitchen window. But all husbands know this instinctively.

What some husbands don't know is that hammocks should be hung so that the occupant of the hammock is facing away from any nearby grass.

There is some law of nature that causes grass to grow visibly when viewed from a hammock.

Then there's that little cloud of gnats that always ac-
companies any country dog.

Hammocks must hang no less than a foot higher
than one's tallest dog.

Ain't science wonderful?

*April 1986*

I'm taking a week of vacation next week and I plan
to spend at least part of it gearing up for summer at
Elam.

That's not an easy task by any means. It takes planning, careful planning.

For one thing, I have to practice my summer gaits,
ambling, moseying, and sauntering.

After all, I do very little moseying, ambling, or sauntering in the winter when it's cold.

No, the step I use in the winter is the Chicago
quickstep which is designed to get one from one's car
to the nearest warm structure in as little time as possible.

The Chicago quickstep is one I learned up north
which entails parking one's car upwind of the said warm
structure, so that one can run with the wind toward that
warm structure, thus reducing by some degree the chill
factor.

The Chicago quickstep is similar in appearance to
the Ozark Mountain green apple quickstep, but used
for a different purpose altogether. The initiated will recognize the difference by the intensity of the look of
urgency on the quickstepper's face during the perform-
ance.

Then, there's the matter of lost tools.

I believe I have successfully lost all the tools that
might conceivably be needed for any of the projects

my wife has mentioned over the course of the winter. But I plan to check out the locations in which I lost those tools and be sure that they are still lost.

Wives are a funny race of people you know, and I have a talent for stumbling over a tool at the most inopportune times, like when the weather's just right for testing a hammock.

So, as you can see, it'll be a sort of a working vacation.

I hope I'm up to it.

*April 1986*

I read an interesting article in Discover Magazine on the subject of tech-speak.

Tech-speak, as it turns out, is that language that technical writers and congressmen often use to tell us what we need to know in a way that we can't possibly understand it.

It's been around for a long time.

Some of the tech-speak that lawyers use to befuddle the masses has been around since the Norman Conquest.

But this article wasn't designed to strike out at tech-speak, or a call for its abolishment, or anything like that; it was designed to give us mere mortals a hand up in understanding tech-speak. And teach us how to use it from time to time to befuddle the befuddlers among us.

For example.

If something is new you can call it enhanced, or advanced, or if it's similar to something else you can refer to it as isomorphic, or allotropic if it's different, or homogeneous if it's mixed with something.

You see the technique.

Whatever you want to say or describe, just get out a dictionary and find another word for it, the longer the better.

A good place to practice might be on your tax return.

Claim damages to your passive solar illumination assembly.

Tell them a probably negative geotropic lithophyte containment device was manually propelled in a transverse direction, thus rendering the vertically installed moisture resistant photon transmission surfaces gaseous exfiltration qualities inoperative.

By the time they figure out that somebody threw a flowerpot through your window, the statute of limitations will have run out.

*April 1986*

I'm telling you folks, this running for president isn't all a bed of roses.

I was reading the New York Times today and they carried a story about Mike Dukakis, who's now the governor of Massachusetts, but wants to be president.

Now, you may remember, that when I decided to run for president here awhile back, I just said so in this space.

I don't remember the exact quote but I think it was something like... "I believe I'll run for president," or something like that.

But the Dukakis announcement worries me a tad.

He's a Massachusetts Democrat. And Massachusetts Democrats know just about all there is to know about politics. And Dukakis didn't just tell folks he's running for president; he announced in New Hampshire, then he went to Boston and announced again, then to Atlanta where he announced again, then to Des Moines,

Iowa, where he announced again; and finally, wound up in New York City where he announced for a fifth time, all in one day.

I don't know what sort of president he'd make. But he'd be a heck of a good airline steward.

Personally, I think I'd have announced just in New Hampshire, or wherever I happened to be, and then borrowed a pocketful of quarters from somebody and called around to all those other places in case they hadn't heard I was planning to run.

Actually, they should have known anyway, since Governor Dukakis announced back on the fourteenth that he was going to announce yesterday (4/29/87).

If I'd known politics was going to involve all this running around I might never have thrown my hat in the ring in the first place. But I always believe in finishing what I start. I'm in the race to the bitter end.

In fact, I think I'll go to Elam this weekend and practice up on my John F. Kennedy impression...

*April 1987*

One of the surest ways on earth to get an argument started in almost any group of people is to bring up the question of nuclear power.

Not the nuclear power of rockets and other war-making machinery, but the production of electric power through the use of nuclear power plants.

Almost every civilized society does it and just about every one of them is opposed, sometimes violently, by people who believe that nuclear energy presents the world with unacceptable dangers.

This past weekend, the first anniversary of the Chernobyl disaster in the Soviet Union presented the opponents of nuclear power with a grand opportunity to speak out and demonstrate their opposition.

And they did, by the thousands, all across Europe, several places in the United States, in Japan.

In Hyde Park in London, one of the more tightly organized groups opposing the use of nuclear power used thousands of participants dressed in special colors to form an enormous radiation danger signal.

And well they might, because the radiation cloud from Chernobyl made vast tracts of English farmland iffy at best as a source of food.

Eastern and western Europe suffered, but most of the western European demonstrations were directed, not at the Soviet Union, but at western European power plants.

The case was similar in the United States and Japan.

Oh, in Moscow, Chernobyl was marked, too.

They had a show about the heroism of the Soviet crews which brought the Chernobyl fires under control and reassured everybody that there will be no long-term health risks.

Oh yes, and there was a demonstration in Moscow, too, against nuclear power...

The eight participants were allowed to have their say.

After all, this is the new era of openness in the Soviet Union.

*April 1987*


With my presidential campaign running along quite smoothly, the thought of withdrawing from the race hadn't entered my mind, until today.

After all, I'm piling up votes by the dozen. My campaign funds are holding out, which is to say I don't have any money for the campaign; but I'm not spending any of it either.

Few politicians are in such an enviable position. The press isn't even speculating on whether I've ever changed my name or lied about my age.

Yessir, things are going well and I ordinarily wouldn't think of quitting the race, but today I did.

Think of quitting the race, that is...

I'm thinking of dropping out and throwing my support behind Senator Bill Bradley of New Jersey.

It's not because he's a former basketball star, and it's certainly not because he's a democrat; but Bill Bradley wants to bring back geography. Says we can't expect to be a world leader if we don't know where the rest of the world is.

And we don't. We don't even know overmuch about where we are.

Bradley commissioned a poll here a while back that showed that most high school students and an alarming number of college students couldn't name three countries in South America, or find Vietnam on the map; a quarter of the students polled in Dallas, Texas, didn't even know what country borders on the United States in the south. And fewer than half the college students polled in North Carolina didn't know that Alaska and Texas were our largest states.

Forty years ago and then some, I studied all that stuff. Course, that was before Alaska was a state. But we all did and a lot of us kept up with the changes in geography since then, and why they took place.

If Bill Bradley wants to bring back geography, I'm for him. Maybe I can get him to say a kind word for history while he's at it.

*April 1987*

I've never gotten into the debate over whether there should or should not be a change from standard to daylight-saving time.

It's always been a problem for me, but I've stayed out of the fight.

My problem isn't that I can't adjust from one time to another, I can. And though I resent losing an hour in the spring when the clocks have to be set forward, I find that resentment tempered in the fall with the realization that I'm getting an extra hour when the clocks go back to standard time.

My problem is that I know there's a clock somewhere that didn't get set forward an hour last Sunday night. And sometime in the next few weeks I will rely on that clock to tell me what time it is, and it will lie to me, and I'll be the better part of an hour late for something.

It happens every year.

And each year it's a different clock, or watch that leads me astray.

And it keeps getting worse.

Now that everything comes with a clock on it, there are clocks on radios and telephones and in cars and on tape recorders and on television sets and on picture frames and pen and pencil sets and cigarette lighters, it's endless.

I spend the better part of that Saturday evening each April setting all the clocks I can think of, and some that I just run across during the hunt through the house. But I know, I just know there's one lurking somewhere that I didn't set. Or that somebody else didn't set. And that I will, sometime in the next few weeks, mindlessly rely on that particular clock or watch and be an hour late for something.

Personally, I think an extra hour of daylight during the winter would be nice and that Congress should decide on one good, reliable time — and stick with it.

Course, I would like to get that hour back.

*April 1987*

Back in the early seventies, Spiro Agnew, who was vice president at the time, referred to the media as the nattering nabobs of negativism.

Spiro wasn't much of a vice president, I'll admit, but he sure could turn a phrase.

When you've been called a nattering nabob of negativism it rules out doubt. You know that the utterer of that phrase holds you in low esteem, or in plainer terms, he flat don't like you. You don't have to wonder about where he stands.

I never cared to think of myself as a nattering nabob of negativism, but I did appreciate the fact that when Spiro Agnew set out to insult somebody he did it efficiently.

Nowadays,you hardly know if you're being insulted or not and words are used that have different meanings, depending on who's using them.

Take the words "liberal" and "conservative" for example.

It used to be that you could describe somebody as either a liberal or a conservative and he wouldn't mind, since either term referred to a perfectly legitimate position in the political spectrum.

But nowadays, if you call a fellow a liberal he may take it to mean that you think he's just a step or so short of being a card-carrying Marxist; or somebody labeled a conservative, depending on the labeler, may feel he's been called a fascist or worse.

I have, in recent weeks, seen the same Washington

based political organization described as a liberal study group and a left-wing think tank.

Flip the coin over and you can have a conservative political action committee become a right-wing pressure group.

I have, in times past, thought of myself as a liberal and as a conservative.

*May 1985*

When Mikhail Gorbachev went on television in Moscow to reestablish his image as the Soviet version of "the great communicator," he fell a little short of the mark.

There were several misstatements of fact — that's a diplomatic term for "lies" — but perhaps the most serious one was his description of the Chernobyl accident as "the first revelation to the world of the sinister force of nuclear energy that has escaped control."

That's not only a lie, it's a weak, ridiculous, and cynical lie.

But don't be offended. He didn't mean it for us. He meant it for his own people.

The purpose of that particular lie was to try to head off the anger of his people when they finally realize that the Soviet Government has ignored some of the most basic safety measures in going ahead pell-mell with their nuclear power industry.

If Chernobyl demonstrates anything, it demonstrates the fact that the Soviet Union counts rubles, the rubles it would cost to build containment buildings and safety devices, as being worth more than the safety and health of the socialist working class.

He also wants his people to believe that the American people didn't learn about Three Mile Island for months.

And, he wants credit for suggesting a rapid reporting

and information exchange on matters of nuclear energy that the United Nations has been trying, and failing, to get the Soviet bosses to do for years.

In this speech we also learned that, in addition to a lot of malicious lies about the Soviet Union, the United States groundlessly accused Libya of involvement in terrorism.

The only thing we actually learned is how one well dressed Russian pronounces Chernobyl.

*May 1986*

I found in the New York Times a long and scholarly article on the subject of peanut butter.

I thought I already knew a lot about peanut butter — I've eaten it all my life. But there were a few facts that I had missed.

For example, did you know that six hundred million pounds of peanut butter are eaten annually, most of it by Americans?

That's about eight pounds per person.

I don't know if I eat that much these days, but I believe I probably ate much more than that in times past. So it evens out.

That wasn't a big surprise.

What did surprise me was to learn that both William Buckley and former President Gerald Ford eat peanut butter for breakfast.

For breakfast.

What's worse, there's a French chef in New York, whose name I can't pronounce, who used peanut butter in a cream sauce that I can't pronounce, and pours that cream sauce over a veal dish that I can't pronounce.

I'm sorta glad too, because if I could pronounce it, I might be tempted to order it, just to show off.

Then there was the line about Julia Child who's supposed to know more about food than us ordinary mortals.

She eats peanut butter on potato chips.

The article didn't say how she gets the peanut butter spread on those potato chips without crumbling them.

It was suggested in this article that port wine is a good accompaniment for peanut butter sandwiches.

It was long about then that the article lost me.

So I searched ahead to find out if they had any information on the only thing most of us really need to know about peanut butter.

I thought so — not a word about how to keep it from sticking to the roof of your mouth.

*May 1986*

A few weeks ago, Gary Hart lashed out — political candidates do that you know, lash out; at least journalists always describe them as lashing out when they say something bad about somebody else, particularly if that somebody is a political opponent.

Anyway, I digress.

As I said, a few weeks ago, Gary Hart lashed out at unnamed political opponents...

Incidentally, when you're going to lash out, it always is safer in politics to lash out at unnamed people, especially if you can't prove the bad things you're saying about them.

But I digressed again.

I do that a lot, digress...

But I was talking about Gary Hart, a few weeks ago...

Well, actually, I was talking about him just a few seconds ago, about how he lashed out a few weeks ago at unnamed political opponents who, he said, were spreading rumor and innuendo about him.

Now, it's a political principle that, if somebody says something about you that you don't want other people to believe, you characterize it as rumor and innuendo, or in some cases, half truths.

Politicians like the term half truth since it leaves you with the possibility that somebody may actually be telling the truth about you, but it's not really what it appears to be.

But, I believe I digressed again.

What Gary Hart was upset about was that these unnamed political opponents were spreading rumor and innuendo to the effect that he was a womanizer.

Now, he's all upset because a newspaper in Florida has done what he said his critics on the womanizing question should do, follow him.

I'm not sure the evidence the Miami Herald gathered would prove the womanizing question. But, I am sure that Gary Hart's actions prove he's not real good at running for president.

*May 1987*


Well folks, it starts tomorrow, and it promises to be the best show since Watergate.

The Iran-Contra hearings begin in Washington and all three networks as well as the Public Broadcasting System want to be sure that you don't miss a thing.

In addition, Cable News Network will have gavel to gavel coverage and C-Span will replay it in the evening.

Yessir, if you're interested at all, there will be no excuse for you not to know every juicy detail of who did what, and with whom, and what did the president know, and when did he know it.

Now, you'd think that the folks who run the major networks might get together and make some sort of an agreement to cover the hearings on a rotating basis.

After all, four days a week for three months or so, is a long time to carry a program that doesn't exactly lend itself to a lot of commercial interruptions.

Then there's the soap operas and the game shows.

But, CBS, and NBC, and ABC want you to believe they're highly responsible and interested in your getting the word on who did what and when did the president know; and they know you don't want to wait till six thirty or so for the highlights, which you'll get anyway.

The real reason they'll all vie to cover the hearings simultaneously is because they all want the star witnesses.

Anybody who's been in this business for more than five minutes can tell you that a cooperative agreement might result in one network having Oliver North, one of the key figures, or Fawn Hall, who may be to Iran-Contra what Maureen Dean was to Watergate, and the others, in their turn, having to settle for somebody like Caspar Weinberger who may be a central character, but has little sex appeal.

At this "point in time," I'm already bored.

*May 1987*


I'm telling you folks, scandals are coming at us these days faster than anyone can be expected to handle them.

Iran-Contra was bad enough, what with all those arms and Arab weapons merchants, and all that...

Then, about the time we had that scandal in shape for the Congress to hold two or three more months of hearings on it, here came the Jim Bakker affair. Some wags are calling it Pearlygate.

Then that one, which started out merely as a case of a preacher misbehaving with a church secretary — bad, but not unknown in the history of the ministry —

snowballed into a case of corporate takeover in the television ministry; and millions of dollars at stake.

I must confess, the idea of a preacher being paid as much as a baseball player scandalized even me. I don't think they should take a penny more than, say, a network anchorman.

You'd think that would be enough scandal to handle at one time.

But no.

On the same weekend we hear that former Governor Robb may have gone to some parties where cocaine was used, and that presidential candidate Gary Hart may have engaged in some extramarital, extracurricular activities.

Scan any newspaper and you're likely to find a dozen or more small, pocket-sized scandals, people taking money in real estate scams, phony travel clubs, insider trading on Wall Street.

It's getting to the point that I don't know what to be indignant about any more.

Or even what to be shocked about.

It's getting tough to even be surprised by some of the things we hear.

I guess it's nothing really new.

It must have been a century ago that Mark Twain noticed that man is the only animal that blushes, or that has any reason to.

*May 1987*

At the beginning of last week, before the Iran-Contra hearings started, I allowed as how I was bored already.

Then, as the week wore on, and I watched and listened to the testimony unfold, both as it happened and in the innumerable recaps on various news programs including this one, I realized that bored was not really a strong enough term.

It's not that I don't think it's important. It is.

If laws were broken, or if the security of the country was threatened, or if the policy of the country was undermined, for patriotic or monetary purposes, I think the American people should know that.

It's one of the strengths of this democracy of ours that we do have the mechanisms, judiciary and congressional, to look out after our interests.

But, if I understand the way this Iran-Contra hearing was prepared, most if not all of the information available to us over the next three months has already been developed in preceding investigations; and the televised hearings are largely to repeat it to us, bit by agonizing bit.

I'm not sure that's necessary.

I'm sure it's boring.

I'm just not sure it's necessary.

At least not necessary in terms of what we ordinary citizens can, or will, do with the information.

It seems to me that if certain parties misbehaved, and need to be indicted or impeached, or whatever, the Congress is perfectly qualified to do that whether the great mass of the American people is looking on or not.

You know, they could handle it the same way they handle a congressional pay raise...

I guess I'd feel a little better about it all if I didn't think it was, in itself, a covert operation...

A way to campaign for office without appearing to.

*May 1987*


From time to time people ask me if I am a Republican or a Democrat. And I always answer quite frankly that I am.

I guess that's not exactly true, since I have never held a membership card in either the Republican or the Democrat Party. But I take the question to mean, how do I vote?

Since I have, over the course of years, voted for people in both parties that I judged to be the right ones for the job in question, I feel perfectly justified in telling people who ask that I am indeed, either a Republican or Democrat.

The question gets a little harder to answer when folks ask if I am a liberal or a conservative.

The problem is, I'm not too sure what defines a liberal or a conservative. So, in order to answer the question, I need to know first what the questioner thinks.

You see the problem.

If the questioner is a liberal, and I turn out not to accept some part of the so-called liberal agenda that he does accept, he may decide that I am a conservative; or it could happen the other way around.

Labels have always bothered me.

Some people who would like to see nuclear weapons eliminated, whether or not there are safeguards guaranteeing that the other side does the same, are in my thinking wrong. But I respect their right to think that way.

Where I have trouble is when they assume for themselves the title, the peace movement or the anti-war movement, thus implying that those who believe in a strong defense are in favor of war.

Then, we have the hawks and the doves. The terms are self-explanatory and they explain precisely nothing.

I believe I'm gonna start a new movement — the Conservo-liberal Republicrats — devoted to a policy of middle of the road extremism.

Argue with that.

*May 1987*

Russell Baker pointed out, rightly I think, in his column that we are in for a new era of full disclosure.

He remembered that we never had to know absolutely everything about a president's health until President Eisenhower went public with his heart attack back in the sixties.

Since then, every time a president gets sick, or even if he's trying to head off a sickness by elective surgery, we are treated to endless details and diagrams.

That's true.

I imagine more American students are aware of the geography of the president's lower intestinal tract than they are of Africa...

Prior to Eisenhower, it was considered impolite to ask another person, even a president, about the particulars of his state of health.

Most Americans were unaware that President Franklin Roosevelt was unable to walk and they were certainly unaware that he had a mistress.

Now, thanks to the Hart incident, not only health but personal moral conduct is grist for the journalistic mill.

Baker thinks future politicial candidates will have to add a morals consultant to their staffs to advise them on looking clean, but not so clean that they come off as wimps.

What's a poor political office seeker to do?

Ellen Goodman asks the question, now that women are making inroads into presidential politics, what we call one who strays from the campaign trail to the primrose path.

A manizer...

Sounds clumsy to me. But now that candidates have to expect to be asked about the state of their moral health, we need to have our euphemisms ready.

And maybe, just maybe, find time for a question or two about foreign policy and the national debt.

*May 1987*

The next time you lose something in the mail, or it gets to where it's supposed to be somewhat late, you may be inclined to get hot at the U.S. Postal Service.

But consider how bad things might be.

You might be a citizen of the Soviet Union, waiting for your shipment of gravel.

According to the New York Times, somebody misplaced a twenty-eight-car freight train loaded with gravel back in 1983 and they haven't been able to find it since.

All they know is that the train, twenty-eight fully loaded cars, left a place called Tomashgorodsky in the Ukrainian Republic back in June of 1983, bound for the Russian Republic by way of the Byelorussian Republic. But it never got to where it was supposed to be.

Ukrainian, Russian, and Byelorussian bureaucrats have been looking for it ever since; but it seems that in the Soviet Union, some records are not kept for more than a year. So the papers that might show where that train and all that gravel might be located, no longer exist.

Now, in this country, where dealing with the bureaucracy is sometimes frustrating, those who need their train or their gravel, would probably send somebody out to look in all the places that a gravel train might conceivably be, and keep looking until they find it.

Not in the Soviet Union. If it ain't on paper it's not there, simple as that. And the only thing now is to find somebody to blame.

I think I know the problem.

The State owns everything in the Soviet Union.

If *somebody* owned that train or that gravel, it'd turn up by Wednesday.

*June 1985*

I fooled around yesterday (6/2/86) and missed a chance to see history in the making.

The United States Senate went on TV.

I could kick myself.

Well, actually no, I couldn't kick myself; I tried once and missed, but you get the idea. I was somewhat miffed with myself for missing the opportunity to turn on a television set here in Hampton Roads and watch what the United States Senate is doing in Washington.

The only thing that makes me feel somewhat better about the whole thing is that most of the United States Senate missed it, too.

According to the Washington Post, only ten of the hundred senators were in attendance on this historic day when the United States Senate finally recognized a technology that's been around for several decades.

The rest were still on their Memorial Day recess.

But they'll come drifting in anyday now and we can expect to see what it is that senators do when they're not conducting hearings or running for president.

I understand yesterday's show was somewhat less than lively.

The New York Times didn't even mention it until page 16 of today's paper, and, if anything of substance took place on the floor of the Senate, the Times, the Washington Post, and several columnists missed it.

Senator Byrd of West Virginia, who at least looks like a senator, is said to have quoted Tennyson, Wilson, and Talleyrand in his praise of the fact that the Senate is now extending its galleries to the world.

Several experts believe, since the cameras are high looking down, that senators with hair will come off better than senators without.

We know they can act — they got elected. The question is, can they reform the tax system?

*June 1986*

I hope it rains soon.

Serious farmers need it for their soybeans, peanuts, and corn and so on - and I need it for my chanterelles.

Chanterelles are a small mushroom that are among the most tasty on the planet and they grow in the woods of Elam in wet weather in July and August.

I found them there several years ago.

At least, I believed that I had found chanterelles.

My wife, who is from Luxembourg where chanterelles are considered a delicacy, thought so, too. But these were a different color from those she remembered from the woods of Luxembourg. So we didn't eat them right away.

Nossir, we looked them up in a mushroom book and discovered that they were almost identical in every way to the chanterelles described in the book.

But we still didn't eat them.

We just continued to walk in the woods and spot them from time to time, and speculate on how much they looked like chanterelles, and my wife would tell mouthwatering stories about how good they are, sautéed — that's a fancy name for fried — with butter, or adorning a steak.

But we didn't eat them.

Finally, I couldn't stand it any longer and had her prepare a portion of these possible chanterelles and see if they still looked like chanterelles after cooking.

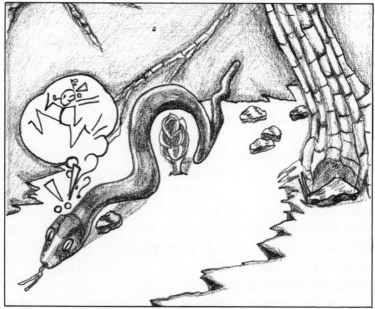

*Actually, the snake was only going to sun himself when Jim took off.*

My wife confirmed that they not only looked like chanterelles but smelled like them, too.

But we still didn't eat them.

We went outside to reread our mushroom book to see if anything that looked anything remotely like a chanterelle was deadly.

While we were doing that, a houseguest wandered into the kitchen and ate what he believed was a leftover dish of chanterelles.

That was on Saturday. On Sunday we all had chanterelles.

*June 1986*

Every so often I get to feeling guilty about never exercising and resolve to do something about it.

Actually, I don't feel too guilty because I do exercise on a regular basis, but I just don't do the exercises recommended in all the diet and self improvement literature that's all the rage in recent years.

Jogging's out.

I don't believe in running in hot weather. It's not good for you.

I don't believe in running in cold weather. You might get a cramp.

Running in moderate weather is less dangerous, of course, but it's just not for me.

I tried tennis here a while back. But people kept returning my serve, mostly to a part of the court so far away that I never had time to walk over and hit it back.

Besides, jogging and tennis are too public.

I prefer to exercise quietly and privately at home, by running a warm bath, soaking awhile, then pulling the plug and fighting the current.

When I'm at Elam, way out in the country, and feel in need of a workout, I often get a lawn chair and go out in the backyard under a big catalpa tree and chase the shade.

I've been known to stay at that for an entire afternoon without stopping.

But what the heck, an exercise program won't do you a bit of good unless you stick with it.

But it won't be long before the blackberries will be ripe and I can get my exercise by picking enough for a cobbler.

Sometimes I pick enough for two cobblers.

Of course, sometimes I see a snake.

On such occasions, I briefly shed my prejudice against jogging.

For twenty yards or so it seems the thing to do.

*June 1986*

This being its two hundredth birthday year, the Constitution is getting a lot of attention lately.

I saw an article in the Washington Post today (6/1/87) about the mean-spiritedness of some of the delegates to the convention that wrote the Constitution.

Some scholars wonder at the fact that a document that has very efficiently served to keep our democracy afloat for two centuries could have been produced by a group of men, many of whom had very little use for democracy or trust that the people could be left alone to operate one.

Supreme Court Justice Thurgood Marshall recently opined that the Constitution wasn't really much of a document at all, since it left slavery and sex discrimination in place.

But, as despicable as those two American institutions

were, one has to wonder if there might not have been another revolution then and there if the delegates had written a Constitution that abolished them then and there, and wonder what might have come out of that second revolution.

Personally, I think our generation is pretty lucky that things happened as they did, no matter our race or sex, since the Constitution turned out to be a working model for a type of government that can, when it wants to, change and modify according to the will of the people.

I don't think those aristocrats who gathered in the summer heat two centuries ago had us particularly in mind as beneficiaries.

At least some of them didn't believe the Constitution, or democracy, would last.

And, they did leave some holes in the contract, some that have been filled, some we may need to fill, and some we probably haven't discovered yet.

But, on the whole, who among us would care to live with what might have been if they'd stayed home and fanned themselves?

*June 1987*

George Will, an able journalist, has some of the same doubts about our mutual profession that I have.

He's referred to it in the past as the indignation industry.

His column on that subject some time ago pointed out that a great many reporters simply can't find happiness in any event that doesn't give us something to be indignant about.

For example, the president's speech the other day to the big AIDS conference.

You may have noticed that the president was soundly booed by at least some in the audience when he suggested routine testing among high risk groups.

What you may have heard about, in the story somewhere, but certainly didn't see, was that the president, in that same speech, was interrupted several times by applause.

But, the casual viewer, who didn't take the time to study the story, could be forgiven for coming away with the impression that the president presented nothing but bad ideas in that speech. Or, more to the point, ideas that were considered bad by that particular audience, or, even more to the point, ideas that were considered bad by some highly vocal members of that audience.

What caused me to wonder if the story aired by the networks, and therefore by local stations, was really fair was watching Nightline last night during which a spokesman for the American Civil Liberties Union disparaged both the Administration's program and its motives in the matter of AIDS, and AIDS testing; then proceeded to endorse a program that was almost precisely identical to the one he condemned.

It was clearly the case of an idea being bad because of the author, not because of the idea.

I don't see any real profit in that for our society or for the battle against AIDS in particular.

We need facts, with the political wrappers off, so we can examine them.

*June 1987*


I've admitted in this space before, and I'm admitting it again right now, I do not understand the science of economics.

I can't even balance a checkbook, my wife does that.

But, even if I could grasp the art of making a checkbook come out even, I would still be a long way from any useful understanding of the science, and the laws of economics.

Anyway, I saw on the front page of the New York Times today that the dollar is declining in value, and, I figured, that's bad.

But no, the Times says that the decline of the dollar is good. That it gives us a trade advantage in foreign markets and that we may not need to worry about the trade war with Japan.

Well, that came as a relief. Because I figure that if Japan should come out as well in a trade war as they came out in the last shooting war we had with them, that we really couldn't afford it.

Like I said, I don't understand it, but it seems that the damage done to our trade balance by Japan was the result of their making premium products and selling them here at bargain prices.

Nowadays, however, the Japanese are making premium products all right, but they're selling them here at premium prices.

Meanwhile, we're selling the Japanese products such as air conditioners, that are premium products. But, with the decline of the dollar they are buying them at prices that are lower than what they can buy a Japanese air conditioning product for.

One Japanese air conditioning manufacturer, for example, has had to go out of business, submerged by a sea of cheap foreign imports.

Sound familiar?

If that doesn't make you any happier, there is a story in the Wall Street Journal about the increased Japanese taste for large American gas guzzling cars...

I think we've got 'em this time, folks, I think we've got 'em...

*June 1987*

Much of the commentary in our nation's newspapers and on radio and television news or talk shows has focused on sex lately.

Back in the fifties, when I got into this business, you couldn't even say the word sex on the air, much less talk about it.

But, we thought about it back then, probably no more or less than people do these days; we just tended to talk less about it.

Maybe that was unhealthy.

On the other hand, maybe it wasn't...

I don't know for sure.

We didn't have AIDS to worry about in those days; but we did have syphilis and gonorrhea to worry about. And then, as now, there was a great debate on how to handle the situation.

If we taught the kids about the venereal diseases they risked getting through casual, promiscuous, or pre-marital sex, might we not also teach them more about how to go about things and get away with it...

Where I went to school, the boys were lectured by the coach, or physical education teacher, and the girls were given the facts usually by the home economics teacher.

I sorta believe it worked, for some, since it seems to me that we had fewer adolescent pregnancies and hardly any venereal disease.

Of course, I could be wrong about that because we didn't talk about it.

I don't know.

But, with the human tragedy of too early parenthood, and the deadly tragedy of AIDS staring us in the face, I wonder if talking about it is really the answer, or if we're talking about the right things.

Pick up any newspaper or magazine these days, and chances are there will be more information about sex, and its consequences, than any former generation ever had; then there's TV, radio, the information's available, whether we do it in school or not.

So why isn't it working?

Do you suppose it could be that we talk too much about sex and too little about values?

*June 1987*

With all the coverage that's been concentrated, and continues to be concentrated, on the Iran-Contra affair, we might hope that another human story doesn't get completely lost in the shuffle.

It has been lost on some people.

I've read several letters to the editor and heard any number of political commentaries in recent days that characterize the Contras in Nicaragua as bandits, loyal to the former dictator Somoza, and the Sandinistas as a band of pure hearted socialists trying to make life better for the peasants.

Bull...

I highly recommend a news story on the front page of the New York Times today (6/17/87) by James Lemoyne.

In it, he details the forcible removal, in just the past month, of more than six thousand peasants from their ancestral homes.

He details the shabby conditions these peasants — peasants, folks, not landlords — the shabby conditions they have to live in, in relocation camps, and their fears that the required reeducation of their children will destroy, forever, the principles they would like their children to learn.

It's a sad story.

It's similar to the story already played out with

thousands upon thousands of Miskito Indians earlier on, and similar to the Soviet enforced relocation and reeducation of thousands in Afghanistan, and similar to the programs being carried out in Vietnam, and Cambodia, and Laos, and...

The world forgot in a hurry the fact that the United States, after taking Grenada away from the gang that stole it, gave it back to the people of Grenada.

I've searched quite in vain for an example of the Marxist-Leninist gang ever giving back any liberty that they have successfully wrested from the people.

I guess it's none of my business. But it seems to me if we're going to assist them in their program, we might do well to look realistically at what that program is.

Not what they say it is.

What it is.

*June 1987*

A friend told me the other day that since I announced my candidacy for president, but didn't specify a party whose banner I would carry, that I may rightly consider myself the front runner in an anonymous party.

That may be, but I don't put too much store in being a front runner.

Gary Hart was a front runner. And look where it got him.

But, about party identification, it's not that I have anything against either the Democrats or the Republicans, it's just that I'm not sure what it means to be either a Democrat or a Republican.

True, the Republicans appear, at a distance, to be rather more conservative than the Democrats, and vice versa, but I can lead you to certain Republicans who are so liberal they could pass for Democrats, and Democrats so conservative they could pass for Republicans.

What's a poor middle-of-the-roader to do?

In England they have Conservatives and Liberals, and Labourites, and Socialists, and they have the decency to have an identifiable political party for them to belong to.

The Germans do, too. If a German is a member of this party or that, you know where he stands on politics.

The French, well, let's not talk about the French.

But, in this country, the only way you can find out where a person stands is to elect him and then watch him for a few years, and sometimes you still don't know.

Frankly, I think the British system is much more orderly, where the Conservatives run as Conservatives, the Liberals run as Liberals, and so on. And the party with the most elected gets to say who the boss will be, and thus the boss can get at least some of the things done that he, or she, and the party promised to do if elected.

Next to that our system seems clumsy, and imprecise, and infinitely more fun.

*June 1987*


I don't know how you handle the heat at your house. But, if you're not air conditioned, or, if you're like me and don't really care for air conditioning, it may help to sit as still as possible and do some heavy duty remembering.

Of course, it's easier for me to exercise my remembering than it is for some of my colleagues, since I have more years to remember than they do. And better still, I can do some of my best remembering back to the days when air conditioning was less the rule than the exception.

In Russellville, Arkansas, in my youth, the only people

who had air conditioning right in their homes were the rich folks.

As for cars, if you saw a car with driver inside and the windows rolled up in the summertime, you assumed that the driver was either rich and cool, or a very determined and very hot social climber.

Churches were air conditioned mostly by hand, that is to say, the little rack on the back of the pew in front of you, where the hymnals go, was usually supplied in summer with a number of cardboard fans with a picture of Jesus on one side and a funeral home advertisement on the other.

These came in especially handy when they turned off the big electric fans up front so folks could hear the preacher.

People still used front porches in those days for sitting on in the evening.

The Ritz theater was air cooled, sorta, by a big water tower out back. But leaving it into a southern Saturday afternoon was hard to do, especially if your dad was home and you hadn't mowed the lawn yet.

It was nice after such a chore to lunch on cold cornbread and a big glass of cold buttermilk.

Maybe later sleep outside on a pallet...

The initiated know what I'm talking about — the rest will just have to make do with air conditioning.

*June 1987*

A woman viewer called me and asked how my broken collarbone is getting along, and what do I think of the resignation of Paul Volcker.

I said my collarbone is beginning to heal and that I don't know, really, how I feel about the resignation of Paul Volcker.

Then I asked her, who is Paul Volcker anyway?

And she told me, and I said, oh that Paul Volcker. Well, if he's as good as they say he is at managing money and bringing down inflation, we'll miss him.

Then she wondered if I fully understood the economic implications Paul Volcker's resignation may well have for the international monetary system, the strength of the dollar overseas, the soaring deficit, and the balance of trade, not to mention the domestic economy and the financial pressures that may well bring about another inflationary spiral with too many dollars chasing too few goods and a possible overreaction in certain financial circles that could well touch off a deflationary trend, thus driving prices up catastrophically.

I told her I thought I'd take a wait and see position on that, what with a broken collarbone and all, that my doctor wants me to take it easy.

Then she asked me, sort of rudely I thought, if I had the most rudimentary understanding of the law of supply and demand.

Well, I had her there...

I told her that those who have the supply get to make the demands.

I guess the simple beauty of that, if I do say so myself, almost poetic explanation of an economic principle stunned her, because she started sobbing and hung up on me.

I can't say I blame her... Weighty issues like economics take a lot out of me, too.

I sure hope I didn't reinjure my collarbone.

*June 1987*


Yesterday one of our reporters wrote that in heat like this, the only place to be was at the beach.

That, of course, was written by someone who never sat beneath the shade of a large oak, or catalpa, by a small stream, sipping something cool and contemplating...

Not contemplating anything in particular, just contemplating.

Personally, I have never been able to understand why anyone would voluntarily sit or lie in the open sun, on hot sand, with the only possibility of getting cool a nearby body of salt water that may, or may not, contain sharks.

I believe it may have something to do with the view...

Particularly the view of other persons who inhabit the beach.

It's certainly not the bathing suits the young ladies wear.

The bathing suits are hardly big enough to attract any attention at all. No, it's definitely the young ladies themselves.

But, getting back to those sharks. I'm told that there are hardly any sharks in the waters near Virginia Beach, and that what sharks there are, are not the type that have people on their menu.

You go ahead and believe that if you want to. But I happen to know that I once saw a great white shark off the coast of Australia, and that the Pacific Ocean and the Atlantic are connected, and that that particular shark, or members of his family, have had time to get here...

I do not know, of course, that sharks commute. But I also do not know that they do not.

For me, the probability of the presence of sharks in any particular ocean renders that entire ocean unsuitable for swimming. I do not need particulars on where the sharks usually do business.

This is not a rash decision on my part. I contemplated

it, long and hard, under a catalpa tree by a small stream with something cool to sip.

*June 1987*

A long-time viewer called me late last week and complained that I haven't talked about Murphy, or the other dogs at Elam for quite some time.

I said it was because Murphy has been behaving himself lately and hasn't done anything particularly outrageous.

For an Irish setter that is.

But that was last week.

And my wife and I traveled out to the farm at Elam Friday night with a specific plan in mind.

That plan was to climb into bed and let the crickets and whippoorwills and bobwhites and frogs in the creek sing us to sleep, and continue to sleep well into the heat of the day on Saturday.

Well, the crickets and whippoorwills and bobwhites and frogs did their work very well, and going to sleep was no problem.

That was about one thirty or so in the morning.

But, about five thirty, well before the heat of the day I had in mind, I woke up to the sound of insistent barking some distance away.

Now, all my dogs bark, and if somebody is coming they don't know, they all bark at the same time; but Murphy goes looking for something to bark at...

In this case it was my neighbor's cows in a field about a quarter of a mile away.

I also know, from long experience, that once Murphy finds something to bark at, he stays on the job until I find him and reassign him to something else.

In this case I thought it might be better for me to find him before my neighbor did.

So, I got up and dressed and went after Murphy with mayhem on my mind.

But, a quarter of a mile walk on a beautiful morning, and being joined by the other four dogs, public relations departments wagging full blast, well, what's a couple hours' sleep anyway?

*June 1987*


Well, shortly before one in the afternoon yesterday we finally came to the close of phase one of the Iran-Contra hearings.

Fawn Hall was the last witness to tell the joint committee what they already knew about the operation to ransom American hostages in the Middle East, and assist the Contras in Nicaragua.

What with the political season well underway, some of the new household names growing out of this whole mess need some time to either test the waters, announce for office, or campaign, so we will be spared a few days before the opening of phase two.

But, getting back to Fawn Hall, who was Colonel Oliver North's secretary. I was pleased that ABC and CBS recognized that the weight of her testimony was not sufficient to cause them to break into regular programming.

Thus they rose, in my estimation, somewhat morally above NBC, which did interrupt regular programming, and the joint committee which exploited her.

We've known since before the hearings began that Fawn Hall was North's secretary, that she helped him shred some documents he felt were sensitive, and that she's quite pretty.

The joint committee developed the information that Fawn Hall was Oliver North's secretary, that she helped him shred some documents, and that she's quite pretty.

A middle aged man with a wart on his nose with the same weight of information would not have been called to testify. And NBC would certainly not have interrupted a soap opera or game show to show it even if a middle aged man with a wart on his nose and the same weight of information had been called.

I think the question of whether or not Fawn Hall was exploited is one with an easy answer. She was.

And she probably didn't even get a boat ride to Bimini out of the deal.

*June 1987*

Hardly a day goes by that we don't come up with a new disease, or ailment of some sort.

The latest, which was called to my attention by Jane Gardner, is called video palsy.

Video palsy, according to the New England Journal of Medicine, is caused by the prolonged zapping of aliens and such while playing video games.

This, say the researchers, can bring on a tingling, numbness, and weakness in the hands which is a sign of nerve damage and a signal to the player that he needs to kick the video habit.

Well, I have the same symptoms when I try to operate a pocket calculator.

I guess I'm one of those poor souls who will never catch up to whatever revolution is in progress. But even though I stay clear of video games, I believe I am already an unwitting victim of video palsy.

I have never played Pac-Man or Ms. Pac-Man, or gone

electronically winging through the galaxy searching for creatures bent on destroying Earth and running off with all our damsels...

I have watched my daughter and some of her friends play these games from time to time.

I always come away from one of these experiences determined to stick to something within the bounds of my technological expertise, like horseshoes...

But in spite of that, I am quite sure I have video palsy.

In addition to the symptoms described in the New England Journal of Medicine, the last time I operated my pocket calculator I felt myself sinking into a deep depression, mixed with uncontrollable feelings of anger and frustration, compounded with trembling hands and an all over clammy feeling...

I was figuring my taxes at the time.

*July 1984*

I don't usually watch much television on weekends — I have lots of woods and fields to walk in at Elam and five of the finest hunting dogs in the country.

They don't find much, but they can hunt with the best of 'em.

But on Saturday evening, I broke my usual habit and sat down to watch the opening ceremonies of the Olympic games in Los Angeles.

I was glad I did.

It was a spectacle and rarely have I ever seen anything that big and complicated go off with never an obvious hitch.

I heard one of the commentators say that two and a half billion people were watching.

A reporter for Tass, the official Soviet news agency, was watching, too.

I read part of his report this morning.

What he saw was a political spectacle, sort of an advertisement for the reelection of President Reagan and propaganda promoting the United States' wicked anti-Soviet attitude.

Now then, I suppose a biased reporter might be forgiven for seeing a plot in something the rest of us probably interpreted more innocently, but remember the entry of the teams from Communist China and from Rumania.

I would have sworn they got standing ovations.

Not so according to Tass. There were official cheerleaders on hand that roused the crowd to cheer our team and the teams of our NATO allies, but held the crowd to grim silence whenever a team appeared from a nation opposed to U.S. policies.

Of course, in the Soviet Union such a story may wash, even with two and a half billion witnesses elsewhere who know the truth.

Lenin said liberty is so precious it must be rationed.

Apparently, truth is the same sort of commodity.

*July 1984*

Folks, I think we're headed for all kinds of trouble in this country if we don't find some way to deal with the subject of racism logically.

Racism, as I understand it, is a system of beliefs held by some members of one race that all the members of another race are somehow inferior, or evil, or just generally worthy of hatred.

Most Americans think of racism as a bad thing.

But, because of the historical experience of this country, some have come to view racism as something directed by whites toward blacks, and not the other way around.

In the days when slavery was the policy in this country, I'd be willing to bet that a greater percentage of black people hated white people than the other way around.

They had better reason.

That hatred wasn't based on race so much as it was based on oppression.

But we have moved mightily ahead since those days, not as far as we should perhaps, and certainly not as far as we will, and racism is properly being put behind us.

But not far enough behind us.

When a Ku Klux Klansman makes a public statement of hatred for black people, we have no trouble identifying that as racism, but when a black religious leader makes an equally unacceptable attack on whites in general and Jews in particular, some of us have trouble putting that in the category where it belongs — racism.

But in the case of Minister Farrakhan some people are afraid to notice, lest they be branded as racists.

If we really want equality, and most of us do, mustn't we be free to disagree not because of race or religion, but in spite of it? Racism, from any source, is still racism.

*July 1984*

I don't know who it was who first noticed that women are hard to live with, or without...

I tried looking it up in Bartlett's Familiar Quotations, but to no avail.

I did notice that men, all down through the ages,

have noticed the simple fact that when women are on the scene, they can make life difficult and that when they are not, life is difficult anyway.

I got to thinking about this and I've come to the conclusion that it's some sort of a plot.

My wife rarely leaves me alone to shift for myself more than a few hours at a time; and I've figured it out — this is to keep me from discovering the secret that she and all other women share, and that is that the simple things they do for us are not really that simple.

Now then, having endured the hardships of batching it last night, and again this morning, I've come to the conclusion that the mission she and my daughter went on to Nag's Head wasn't really the main thing — the lesson I would learn would be good for me.

What did I learn?

Well, I learned that I do not know how to make a toasted cheese sandwich by myself.

She can put five dishes on the table that require different cooking times, have them all there at the same time, and all hot, and all delicious, and I can't make a toasted cheese sandwich.

I can't even get it out of the toaster.

Even my recipe for cornflakes came a cropper.

My vitamin tablets gave me heartburn.

My feet got cold last night and it's the end of July.

I burned my morning coffee.

I've owned this shirt for four years. Today it doesn't fit.

Would you believe that it's possible to get your socks on the wrong feet?

Being without a wife for a couple of days builds character, if you survive. But why do they have to be so mean about it?

*July 1984*

The national networks noticed something at the Democratic Convention this year that some of us could have told them somewhat earlier.

That being that the main decisions as to what would happen at the convention had already been made, and, from a news standpoint, they could have done just as well with much less effort and manpower, or should that be personpower...

No matter, it seems the heads of the networks were there and decided that much of their employees' efforts were directed toward filling airtime while waiting for something newsworthy to happen.

And, in keeping with that monumental discovery, they're talking about covering future conventions more modestly.

Several of them were quoted today in the New York Times to that effect.

But, don't bet any money on it.

The networks are in competition with one another, and as long as all three, plus the cable services, are vying for your viewership whenever they all cover the same event, they will try to outdo each other.

About the only way to get the networks to do it any other way, would have to be for them to bid for exclusive rights, like for the Olympics and the Super Bowl, which might be a good idea, since the parties always need money to pay off their campaign debts.

I don't think they'll do that either.

No, we'll continue to cover the conventions lavishly, if only to hear what outrageous things politicians can say about each other and still claim to be friends.

Besides, where else could we be treated to the spectacle of what normally sane people will wear on their heads in furtherance of a political cause.

Let them stay, they're an American art form.

*July 1984*

The president and vice president went to Texas and, as anyone who watches American politics as a spectator sport could have predicted, they wore cowboy hats.

Of course, President Reagan comes by the wearing of cowboy hats naturally. He used to wear them in some of his movies and, for all I know, it's Vice President Bush's favorite sort of headgear. But, even if they both were from Boston, and had never seen a cowboy hat before, they would have worn them yesterday in Texas.

That's just one of the things politicians do when there's an election coming up.

This is not a criticism, just an observation.

And, if Walter Mondale and Geraldine Ferraro campaign in Texas, I'll lay odds right now, somewhere along the way they'll slip in a cowboy hat.

Of course, if berets or ball caps, or motorcycle helmets were the national headgear of Texas, they'd wear those as readily as they wear cowboy hats.

It's just another of the creative ways politicians have of trying to tell us that they understand our culture and think well of it, and would like to have us vote for them.

As the campaign wears on, you can expect to see pictures of our leaders and would be leaders in all sorts of garb, and eating all sorts of local delicacies, and paying lip service to all sorts of local boasts and customs, and trying with might and main to convince us that they're enjoying themselves and would have come and worn, and done, and eaten, and praised everything in this particular instance, even if they didn't want to be president, or vice president, or senator or something.

You can't trust 'em, but they're fun to watch.

*July 1984*

There was an interesting story in the New York Times today (7/18/84) about a problem that really shouldn't be a problem but, people being people, will be a problem anyway.

The problem — how shall Walter Mondale and Geraldine Ferraro act toward each other when they appear in public?

In a few hours, he will be the democratic candidate for the presidency and she will be the democratic candidate for the vice presidency, and the campaign will begin.

And the staffers are worried.

For instance, when all the celebrating takes place after the nominations, the candidate team usually hug with one arm and wave with the other.

Is this proper when one candidate is a married man and the other is a married woman?

And, in the course of the campaign, if they appear together, how do they act toward each other?

When people share a common cause, and score a victory, it's only natural to hug each other. Football players and politicians do it all the time. But if Mondale and Ferraro hug, they'll displease some constituents and if they don't, they'll displease others.

Personally, I belong to the pro-hugging school.

I see nothing wrong with celebrating a victory, or a friendship, or common concerns with a bear hug, man or woman, young or old; it makes no difference to me. A hug just seems to me to be a natural and acceptable way to say, "I know how you feel, I feel that way, too."

But, apparently, the staffers have decided that Mondale and Ferraro must be friendly, but distant.

I hope their spouses are there tonight when they achieve perhaps the second finest moment that can come in American political life.

At a time like that, you need to hug somebody.

*July 1984*

They call these, I believe, the dog days of summer.

I heard Len Randolph explain recently that there's an astronomical reason for that, something to do with the location of the dog star Sirius.

I hadn't known that before.

I always thought that the dog days probably were named for days of such summer heat that even dogs moved about in it only when necessary.

That's the sort of weekend it was at Elam.

I got there Saturday afternoon after a morning of grand marshalling at the Hampton 375th anniversary parade.

Grand marshalling takes a lot out of a fellow, so I was prepared to move slowly once I got to Elam.

The dogs were way ahead of me.

We spent most of the late afternoon chasing the shade under a big catalpa tree in the backyard.

Every so often one of them would get up and amble slowly over to the creek and take a drink and then wallow in the cold water for awhile, and come back to where the people were sitting to shake.

It would have been an ordinarily quiet Saturday afternoon if Murphy, our Irish setter, hadn't wandered into the kitchen and noticed the door of the dishwasher was open. And the dishwasher was fully loaded, with the bottom drawer still out and the combination of that weight and Murphy's when he put his forepaws on it to inspect for possible leftovers, tipped the machine forward.

When a full day's worth of china and glassware cascades from a tipped over dishwasher in the quiet of an Elam Saturday afternoon, you tend to notice that.

I didn't actually see Murphy do it, but he was the only dog of the six who didn't come around to watch the cleanup operation.

*July 1985*

*I never did that.*

Ever since I started talking about my farm at Elam from time to time on this broadcast, and that's been more than seven years ago, people have been asking me just where in the heck is Elam anyway?

If I go out in the evening to dinner, or accept an invitation to speak to a club or organization, sometime along the way somebody will ask me, Jim, just where in the heck is Elam, anyway?

I've always tried to be as honest as possible in the answer, telling them that Elam is located roughly half-way between Pamplin and Prospect, and not far from Tuggle. But that's about as precise as I can get. Elam just doesn't happen to be easy to locate, and today, it's even harder to locate.

I'll try to explain that.

The Highway Department put up signs some years ago on Route 460 at that point where the highway passes through Elam, one on one side of the road for eastbound traffic, and one on the other for westbound traffic.

Elam is sort of a slim community.

Anyway, those signs keep disappearing.

Usually one at a time. And usually just the sign. They leave the post there for the Highway Department to put up another Elam sign.

But Saturday night, for some reason or another, somebody came by with a saw and stole both signs, eastbound and westbound; and to add insult to injury, they took the posts, too.

It was all the talk at the Olive Branch Methodist church ice cream social last night.

It's a mystery.

Biggest crime wave we've had at Elam since my Irish setter Murphy came across a fully prepared Perdue oven stuffer roaster that wasn't being watched...

Of course, we know why Murphy did it. But who's taking those signs is a mystery.

*July 1986*

One of the things I generally don't do when I'm on vacation is watch a lot of television.

I have nothing against television, mind you; in fact, I like it a lot and enjoy working in it. But when I'm on vacation I don't watch television for much the same reasons that a dentist on vacation doesn't go looking for some teeth to fill.

But, when the nation's giving itself a party, and celebrating the centennial of the statue of liberty, and most of the action is taking place in New York, and you're the sort of person who once promised himself that if he ever got out of New York in one piece, he'd never go back, then you're sorta stuck with the fact that you've gotta attend the party on television or miss it altogether.

So I watched quite a bit of television these past few evenings.

What a show.

It was, of course, shamefully expensive and blatantly commercial at times, and glitzy, and tacky, and maudlin, and stickily sentimental, and just downright wonderful.

People have been wandering around the office all day today talking about their favorite moments during the celebration, and how proud they were to be Americans, and how they choked up at this scene, or that song. And these are news people, supposed to be hardboiled and tough to impress.

Did you see the classical concert in Central Park Thursday night? Can you imagine, eight hundred thousand people in one place at one time, and not a single arrest...

And how about the fireworks and the ships, and the bands, and the statue, and the swearing in of new Americans?!

I think I must have teared up sixteen or seventeen times, not counting *every* time they played the national anthem.

Yessir, it was quite a party.

*July 1986*

There was an interesting item in the Wall Street Journal the other day, a letter actually, that asked a burning theological question.

At least it's burned in my mind since I was a youngster back in Arkansas, but I never dared to ask it.

The writer, Donald G. Smith of California, raised the question as to whether it's necessary to say grace when one is having meatloaf...

He said in essence that he would, if necessary, eat meatloaf, but he felt uncomfortable thanking the Almighty for it.

Well, he's never eaten my wife's meatloaf. She calls it "pâté", or he would be glad to include it in his saying of grace. But that's another thing altogether.

I know how the man feels.

Ever since I was a tad I have hated broccoli, and I was often called on to say grace when broccoli was present on the table and I felt decidedly uncomfortable being vocally grateful for a meal that included broccoli, when in my heart of hearts I knew that I was ungrateful. And I suspected that the Almighty knew I was ungrateful, and that I was lying.

I was always sorry about the lie; but I was even more sorry about the broccoli, because the price of getting the chicken and mashed potatoes was to live through a helping of broccoli.

I was always glad when Preacher Chadwick came to Sunday dinner.

Naturally, with a preacher at the table I was relieved of the duty of saying grace in favor of a professional.

His graces were almost as long as his sermons. But I was alert when he said them because Preacher Chadwick itemized his graces and thanked the Almighty for each and every dish, except the broccoli.

Of course, preachers could ask for what they wanted while small boys had to take everything.

I sincerely debated going into the ministry.

*July 1986*

When I went on vacation last week, I promised myself that I would let the world get along without me for nine days, and, I'm happy to report I kept that promise.

And sure enough, just as I thought, I came back to work today and found the world in just about the same condition as when I left it.

So, I guess I don't have to feel overly guilty about going to Elam last week and doing just about as nearly nothing as possible.

Well, I did something. I just didn't do anything useful.

I took a lot of walks in the woods with my dogs.

And when I got back from those walks I got into a chair under a big catalpa tree and chased the shade.

I did some ambling and moseying, and occasionally broke into a full scale saunter.

I did have to move onto the porch occasionally to wait for a thunderstorm to pass. But, the thunderstorms were a pleasant break in the hectic routine and I even saw a magnificent rainbow in the wake of one of them that actually reached the ground on one of my fields.

I debated going to the foot of that rainbow to look for the pot of gold that's rumored to be there in some circles. But, I couldn't remember offhand where my shovel was the last time I used it. I couldn't even remember for sure if I had a shovel, and if I did, what sort of condition it was in. And, by that time, the rainbow had gone back to wherever it is that rainbows go. And, besides, it looked like it was about to start raining again, and...

Well, that's just the sort of week it was.

Tired me out so much I feel like I need a vacation.

*July 1987*

Discovery finally got off this morning after three false starts, and I'm sure the folks in the country's space program are breathing easier.

What struck me most about this event was the calm attitude everybody had about it.

Space travel is getting to be old hat.

I got to thinking about that today, how things have changed since the first manned space flight.

I was working this trade in St. Louis during the days of the Mercury series, back when they built the Mercury capsule at McDonnell Aircraft there, and when a shot was taking place the whole world seemed to be watching that event and hardly anything else.

In those days a successful space shot was when the capsule went up with a man aboard and got back to splashdown at sea with no more than a dozen or so heartstopping emergencies.

Nowadays, like today (8/30/84), I doubt if one in a hundred could name all six crewmembers who are up there doing scientific experiments, doing some medical manufacturing, and putting some new communications satellites into orbit.

We have medical technology now that has already saved countless thousands of lives because of our acceptance of the challenge of space.

Our cars and other mundane machines run better because of the technology developed for space, not to mention the growing variety and efficiency of our entertainment and information media.

And to think, less than eighty-one years ago, Wilbur and Orville Wright were elated with a powered flight of less than a minute.

None of us has a choice of when and where to be born.

But if we did, I wonder if it would be possible to beat this century — in this country.

*August 1984*

Author's Note: Author expected one day to have to write a commentary such as that of 1/28/86 (p. 18 ). Progress, like freedom, is not — and has never been — free.


Anne Burford did the Reagan Administration a favor, sort of, and resigned from a job she doesn't really have just yet.

You may remember that President Reagan had some problems with Mrs. Burford before, when she was head of the Environmental Protection Agency.

She was faced with the problem of obeying the order of her boss, the president, or obeying the orders of a congressional committee, and she chose to obey the president.

Congressional committees don't like to be told no — even by the president, so Mrs. Burford became a controversial figure and by and by lost her job at E.P.A.

Nobody ever *established* that she didn't do her job properly, but a lot of powerful folks *said* she didn't. And in Washington, that's sometimes enough to go on.

Anyway, the president recently appointed Mrs. Burford to another job, that of head of the National Advisory Commission on Oceans and Atmosphere.

Immediately, there was a hue and cry from the opposition; but Mrs. Burford helped the other day when she made a speech and described the commission in unflattering terms.

She called it a joke, nothingburger.

That gave her critics ammunition, whether it was accurate or not. I guess she didn't really want the job anyway, I don't know.

But, in that same speech she also offered a description of the nation's capital, Washington D.C.

She said it was too small to be a State and too big to be an asylum.

As a former inmate of Washington, I formed a new opinion of Mrs. Burford...

I hope she gets another chance at a government job; I don't think we can afford to let such keen analytical ability go to waste.

*August 1984*


Well folks, I know this will be hard to believe, but we're about to go into the political season.

That's right. In this country it starts right after Labor Day.

I know, you have the impression that the campaigning for this election started several years ago. But that was just the preliminaries, just the jockeying for position; the campaign itself will begin next Tuesday.

What we've had up till now wasn't the campaign at all. It was just politics.

Politics is one of the things we do well in this country. And what people do well, they tend to do all the time.

Back during the Olympics we heard a lot of talk about how we should keep politics out of sports.

And we hear all the time about how we should keep politics out of religion.

Heck, we can't keep politics out of grocery shopping.

I think it's high time we broke down and admitted what the sociologists and barbers have known all along, that humans are political animals and that we are not likely ever to give up something we love as dearly as we love politics.

If we have to pay more for a widget than we think that widget is worth, we blame the party in power for having given in to the widget lobby,and vow to vote for the other party.

We heartily scorn the polls that say this candidate or that one is in the lead, and would win if the election were held today; then gleefully quote any poll that says our favorite would win, if the election were held today.

The election, of course, will be held in November. That poll will count. It will also mark the beginning of the 1988 election campaign.

*August 1984*

All my life I've heard the phrase "Once in a blue moon."

Thus and such happens but once in a blue moon, you know how it goes.

But it never occurred to me to wonder, at least not enough to research the matter, just what in tarnation a blue moon was.

Now, out of the blue, I was hit with the information last night that we had a blue moon and it was cloudy, and I couldn't see it.

Not that the moon was actually blue.

It was the same color it usually is.

It wasn't an astronomical phenomenon at all, it was more calendrical.

I love to use big words like that.

A blue moon, I learned to my dismay, is when there are two full moons in the same month, and last night's was the second full moon of July 1985, the other one having happened on the second of the month.

That's all.

Nothing very romantic about it at all, even though it only happens about once every three years.

One time in a century or so, that would be romantic, or at least unusual.

I calculate there must have been fifteen or more blue moons just in my short lifetime.

We lost a lot of the romance of the moon when American astronauts started stomping around on it in the sixties and determined that it was definitely not green cheese, but just undeveloped real estate.

Now we learn that a blue moon is just a function of dates on a calendar.

I haven't been so disappointed since I found out a cat couldn't jump over it.

*August 1985*


Ever since I started groveling, whining, and pleading for pity a few days ago, pity for the agony and pain I'm suffering while becoming a non-smoker, reactions have been coming in all forms.

Except pity.

Sure enough, just as I predicted yesterday, I saw my doctor, Hopalong, and while he was a veritable fountain of advice and counsel, not one shred of sympathy.

He actually takes the position that becoming a non-smoker is a favor that I'm doing for myself and that I will be glad that I made such a wise decision.

He didn't say when I'd feel that way, just that I would.

I figure sometime in the early nineties if I continue to make progress at the same rate I've made it over the past six days.

Doctor Hopalong says it won't take that long, that the enjoyment of breathing regularly and the prospect of doing it for a long time to come will one day make my thirty-year-plus love affair with tobacco seem like merely a bad dream.

A number of former smokers have been kind enough to call to confirm that sort of thinking and to congratulate me on deciding to quit smoking.

So, I guess I'll make it, even if I have to do it without pity.

However, if I am going to be a former smoker I guess it's time I decide just what sort of former smoker I'll be.

Some former smokers just have to rub it on their colleagues who still smoke.

They put up "Thank You For Not Smoking" signs and remove ashtrays from their desks, and gaze across the room with a look of infinite sadness at friends who continue to smoke.

As a former smoker, I hate such people.

As a former smoker, I think that's just the sort of former smoker I'll be.

*August 1986*

I read today that the president is in favor of raising the speed limit.

Well, I thought I read that. But further on in the story, after the headline told me that the president wants to raise the speed limit, a more detailed reading revealed that the president is in favor of the States regulating the speed limits within their borders.

He said so in a letter to some senators and congressmen from Nevada and Idaho.

At least they say he did, I don't know for sure, but they seem like honest fellows.

Senator Steven Symms of Idaho says the fifty-five mile an hour speed limit literally wastes a billion hours a year.

Safety experts, on the other hand, say the fifty-five mile per hour limit saves an additional two thousand lives per year.

I suspect both sets of statistics are true, or as true as statistics can be, which isn't very, usually.

West Germany which has no speed limit on its autobahns, reported the same decline in highway deaths after the Arab oil embargo that this country did; their statisticians say it was the lack of fuel that diminished the miles driven that drove the death rate down.

Anyway, these western senators believe, whether the president does or not, that there are plenty of roads in wide open country that could be travelled safely at higher speeds than fifty-five.

As a matter of fact, I agree...

In fact, there's a road between here and Elam that is perfectly negotiable at a speed well beyond fifty-five.

I know, I tried it one afternoon, on an isolated stretch in Dinwiddie County, where I was alone — except for a State trooper, sitting there where no State trooper had ever been in over eight years.

So much for statistics.

*August 1986*

One of the things I enjoyed most about the major parties' national conventions this year was that I didn't have to go to either one of them.

This was the second time in a row that I haven't had to go to either of the national political conventions.

It's not that I don't enjoy politics, I do, it's our national sport; but it's more fun at a distance.

I feel the same way about professional football.

I can understand it better if I'm able to sit at home in front of a television set and see the instant replays.

Football that is...

No amount of instant replays can make politics understandable.

But, it's like football in that an expert on the subject can analyze the facts, show and tell all the reasons that this one particular candidate will win in November, and prove it to the satisfaction of any reasonable observer; and the other guy will win in November.

Economists are that way. Two economists can take the same set of figures and have us in the middle of a remarkable economic recovery or on the edge of a depression.

Personally, I believe most politicians are just economists who can't add.

Anyway, back to the political conventions.

I enjoyed watching them and seeing how far people will go in trying to convince us that their party has all the angels and the other one has all the devils.

They convince me every time.

I guess the best I've ever heard it phrased was during one of the conventions, I won't say which one. After an early evening speech my wife called me:

"I think that was the greatest speech I've ever heard," she said, "and I couldn't help wishing I were eighteen years old again and could believe every word of it..."

*September 1984*

Politicians are a funny race of people.

I keep coming back to that conclusion every election year.

I know it's part of the job of a politician to win whatever election he's participating in, or she's participating in, in some cases.

But don't you get a little tired of hearing that we better vote this way or that in this very upcoming election or the Republic might just as well take down its sign?

I wish they wouldn't make everything seem so final.

The trouble is, I know they're all honorable men and women, and want what's best for us, and tell the truth insofar as that's possible for a politician. So, when somebody has been chosen to bear the standard for his or her political party says something, I listen; and I tend to take what's being said pretty seriously, and I always wind up fearing for my country. Until I hear the other side's answer, which colors my opinion of the first guy, or gal, or whatever. And I continue with my fear for my country unabated except for the direction in which it will slide into perdition, or depression, or nuclear holocaust, or theocracy, or something.

Some nights in recent time, I have lain awake into the wee hours confiding my doubts to the Almighty, and seeking to poll that power beyond our understanding on how to vote this November, when voting either way is a clear mandate for disaster.

I don't think the Almighty's answered me directly. But I did have a vagrant thought pass through my mind during one of these musings, and it could have been the beginning of an answer, I guess — it wasn't signed...

But it went... "...this all takes me back to the time when Franklin Roosevelt was running against Tom Dewey..."

*September 1984*

Folks, I've taken all I can. It's time for a change. We've probably waited too long already, but with faith, hard work and grit, we may still be able to restore some semblance of order to the chaos of recent years.

I'm speaking, in short, of the terrible mess we've made of the English language.

I realize that English, especially the dialect we use here in the United States, has always had shortcomings, but the situation has become more acute in recent years.

It's all these new words...

Most of them unnecessary.

The next time somebody comes around with a new word to describe something that we already have several good serviceable words for, I'm gonna dangle me about three pounds of participles and throw them at him.

Take orientate for example.

Do we really need to waste time orientating people when we could just as easily orient them? Or, and this will probably break some bureaucratic hearts in government, even just *tell* them what they need to know?

I've studied the problem, and figure that in any government report there is an average of more unnecessary verbage than any sane person would have time to count.

Nothing less than open revolt will do. We have to get organized and demand that English be made simple enough for any college graduate to understand with no more than two or three repetitions.

Join me in this new and noble crusade.

Start small if you want to.

If somebody offers to conference with you, tell them you don't have time, but you will talk with him.

Finally, we need some new laws, simple laws, and a good starting point would be one that makes it illegal to add any new word to the English language before we learn to spell the ones we've got...

*September 1984*

There's an old saying in our business, and I try to live by it, but I don't always succeed.

It goes like this...

"...set brain in motion before engaging mouth..."

And I certainly failed to do that a few nights ago when I was searching my mind for a headline, we call it a tease, that would tell folks what we were about to talk about on an upcoming news broadcast.

It happened like this.

Jane Gardner and I were on the set waiting to begin our eleven o'clock report.

A few seconds before the actual broadcast was to begin, the floor director reminded me of something I should have been prepared for, but wasn't. And that was that it was my night to do the tease which was only a heartbeat or so away.

So I did.

When the camera and microphone came on, knowing that we were about to tell you about hurricane Diana and struggling for some way to mention that fact, I engaged mouth while brain remained firmly in neutral, and said, I admit it... "Just like a woman, Diana is keeping us guessing..."

Well, I don't know if you'll understand this, or believe it, but I didn't mean that as an insult to women.

In fact, it is the eternal mystery of women that prompted that vagrant thought and what turned out to be a thoughtless phrase. But I knew immediately that it wasn't something that I would have said if I had thought about it.

And even if I hadn't guessed that, I would have known shortly anyway.

Jane told me so, our producer Dotty Wikan agreed, and a veritable hurricane of calls and letters confirmed it beyond doubt.

I can't promise that I'll never say anything stupid again. But I can reliably assure you I'll never say that particular stupid thing again.

*September 1984*

I guess I'm just going to have to get organized.

A lot of people let important things slide to the last minute, and I'm one of those.

In fact, it's a lifelong habit with me, one of those I developed back in high school with homework.

I would always put off doing it until the last possible moment in the usually vain hope that the teacher would change her mind, that the school would burn down, that I would come down with something incurable, or that, vain hope of all vain hopes, that I would find some completed homework on the way to school that had been done the night before by a student in my class with handwriting similar to mine, but a much better grasp of the subject matter, who, nevertheless, was careless enough to drop it somewhere along the very same route that I took to school.

That hardly ever happened.

Anyway, all this leads up to a couple of notes in my "things to do sooner or later" basket.

One was a note from somebody who knows of a dog that eats concrete blocks, and I've lost the phone number.

Another is a question from a woman who wants to know what kind of winter we'll have based on woolly bear observation. And since I got that note, I have looked high and low for a woolly bear and haven't been able to find one.

For those of you who are not familiar with woolly bears, they are fuzzy little worms with alternating bands of black and brown hair. The width of the bands, or rather one set of the bands, reliably can be used to predict the severity of any upcoming winter. It's either the black bands or the brown bands, depending on who you talk to.

Some people think if the black bands are wider that the winter will be long and severe; but that's not so. It's when the brown bands are narrower. Let me know if you see one.

*September 1984*

Well it appears that mudslinging is safe, for the moment, as a time honored American political institution.

You may remember, a few years ago, some troublemakers in the Congress tried to get some laws on the books that would require politicians to tell the truth about each other.

Such a radical and clearly unimplementable idea was turned back by saner heads in the Senate, of course, but some guys never learn.

Now several senators have introduced legislation that would require television stations to provide free air time for the victim to respond if he, or she, is subjected to mudslinging in paid political advertising.

They call it a clean campaign bill.

That's an oxymoron.

You know what an oxymoron is, don't you?

That's a self-contradicting phrase.

Like Iranian Government or Soviet integrity, or government fiscal responsibility.

A clean campaign bill.

Even if it could be done, where's the challenge, where's the fun?

The way politicians talk about each other has enriched the English language for years, and through it all, Americans have been pretty good at sorting out what's fact and mudslinging and making some fairly good choices.

Anyway.

We're safe.

That bill is being opposed by two very powerful pressure groups...

...the National Conservative Political Action Committee and the American Civil Liberties Union.

Who was it who said — politics makes strange bedfellows.

*September 1985*


I was talking with a friend the other day about the wave of popularity being enjoyed by professional wrestling and he hit me with a strange theory.

He believes wrestling is popular because cowboy movies can't be depended on any more.

"How's that," I asked.

"Simple," he said, "when you and I were kids we could go to the movies on Saturday afternoon and see Roy Rogers, or Gene Autry, or the Cisco Kid, and be confident from the very beginning that good would triumph over evil."

Those movies, he pointed out, always provided us with bad guys who looked like bad guys and good guys who looked like good guys. And the good guys always conducted themselves honorably, no matter how mean and underhanded the bad guys were and no matter how hopeless the situation seemed to be. Sometime during the last few minutes of the picture show, the bad guy would try to get away on a horse. And the good guy would go after him. And after the bad guy ran out of bullets the good guy would put away his gun, drag the bad guy off his horse, and beat the tar out of him, fairly, of course. And never get dirty or lose his hat in the process.

Wrestling matches provide the same sort of morality play.

Evil looks like evil.

Good looks like good.

Evil may appear to get the upper hand, for a time.

But, eventually, wrestling fans know that the big show-down will come and good will prevail.

We just don't know exactly when.

That's what keeps folks coming back to wrestling matches — to be there when justice is done.

We all want revenge sometimes.

Justice is okay in its place, but revenge sells.

*September 1985*

I just love the way economists talk.

I rarely understand what they say, but they say it so well and so colorfully.

I heard a couple of them on David Brinkley's Journal yesterday talking about the new tax law, the new simplified tax law.

Now, I don't know much about the new tax law, or what it will mean to us taxpayers, but I do know something.

What I know is, that now, after listening to those economists, I understand less about the new tax law than I did before I heard what they had to say.

But I don't worry about understanding tax laws anymore. I have a guy, I've told you about Fast Frank, and Fast Frank does my worrying about tax laws for me.

Occasionally, when I hear an economist say something that I think I probably should worry about, I call up Fast Frank and run it by him and he translates it for me into understandable English.

For example, try on this phrase that I found on the front page of the Wall Street Journal...

Quote. The continuation of large structural deficits, combined with shrinkage in the inflow of foreign savings, might conceivably put such pressure on the Federal Reserve that it would finance an expansion in aggregate demand high enough to start a new round of inflation. Unquote.

Frank says that means that this guy doesn't know what's going to happen either, but he's been able to construct a sentence that efficiently disguises that fact.

As to the simplicity of the new tax law, I heard that "the complexity level remains sufficiently high that professional input will be required to obviate unacceptable error levels in personal tax preparation."

I asked Fast Frank what it means...

He said it means he can charge more this year.

*September 1986*

Well finally, after years of debate and indecision the Congress of the United States has settled an issue.

The national flower of the United States of America is — the rose.

They didn't say what color so I guess any rose will do.

One Washington wag said the choice of the rose was particularly appropriate since, even though it's been changed and modified down through the years, the rose has steadfastly maintained a defense system.

That's good enough for me.

Actually, I have to admit to you that I didn't know we didn't have a national flower.

I don't recall it coming up on Jeopardy lately.

I didn't even know we needed a national flower. And now that we have one, I don't know what in the world we're supposed to do with it, or about it.

But it got me to wondering. So I looked in my almanac — I have a 1966 almanac my producer gave me this year — and noticed that almost all the states have a state flower, most of them have a state bird, a few have a state tree, and some have a state animal.

Two or three even have a state rock, or a vegetable.

Now, nationally, we have a national bird — the bald eagle — and, as of yesterday thanks to the tenacity of Congress, a national flower. But have any of those senators and congresspersons we sent to Washington turned their attention to a national animal, or tree, or rock?

I think not.

Nooooo, they've been frittering away their time on tax reform, and world peace, and stuff like that.

For national animal I would propose a horse and we could send one to Washington for Congress to consider an entire horse for a change...

*September 1986*

I don't mind telling you folks I'm a tad disappointed in this country's high leadership.

It's not so much that they did precisely what they said they would not do, and swapped Nick Daniloff for a Soviet spy, but that they did that and then turned right around and said they didn't.

President Reagan was clearly uncomfortable this morning (9-30-86) at a news conference when he told the assembled reporters that the release of Daniloff in the Soviet Union and the release this morning of Gennady Zakharov, after a sham court hearing, were not related.

Of course we got a bonus in the deal with the agreement by the Soviets to release several dissidents sometime soon; but let's be realistic, we get back an honest journalist, or a clumsy spy in the person of Daniloff, and the Soviets get a license to operate a spy network in the United States.

All they have to do when one of their spies is nailed is find an American who happens to be in the Soviet Union at the moment and swap their guy back home before he can do them any damage in a courtroom.

Whatever else was in the deal for Daniloff, that principle was certainly established.

It's one they've used before, and now, since it worked so well again, they'll surely use in the future.

Taking hostages is nothing new for the Soviet Union. They're currently holding thousands of hostages, Jews who want to emigrate to Israel, dissidents who are in internal exile, that is, forced to live under what amounts to permanent house arrest, mental patients whose illness leads them to question the State.

Ransoming Daniloff and the other hostages was probably the decent and humane thing to do. So why can't we just call it what it is?

I can live with a deal, but I don't like to be hustled.

*September 1986*

In case you haven't been keeping track — we've just about used up summer.

Tomorrow morning at a minute before three it will become autumn, the autumnal equinox will take place at that moment.

It may be hard to step outside into the weather and believe that it's autumn, but it is; the calendar and the astronomers say so. And that's that.

Somehow I prefer to learn about autumn in the old way, on the farm at Elam.

There's an edible mushroom that grows in the woods of Elam in great abundance in the summer, but it always quits before autumn.

This weekend I found about twenty of them where I would usually expect to find several hundred, and those twenty were a little on the dry side.

I saw some woolly bear caterpillars, too, but I never can remember what it means, the width of the woolly bear's stripes.

The way I figure it, since my woolly bears don't have any stripes this year, or they're just one solid stripe all the way around from end to end, we're in for a very mild or a particularly severe winter.

Another sure sign of autumn at Elam is the bareness of the tobacco fields. They've been harvested.

Some of my neighbors raise tobacco. And I've watched them do it and wonder why anybody would work that hard on something that's getting to be less socially acceptable by the day.

Then there's the surest sign of all that autumn's here and winter's on the way.

The chimney sweeps in the three chimneys of our old farmhouse will be gone one morning soon and we'll need a fire in the fireplaces that very night.

Calendars are okay and pretty reliable on the whole, but I don't think I'd miss a calendar like I'll miss those little birds.                              *September 1986*

This annual wrestling match in the Virginia Legislature over a state lottery is getting to be a tradition.

In fact, I'm almost afraid the legislature will someday allow the people of Virginia to record their views on the subject, by way of a ballot box, and thus deprive us of some of the best oratory this side of championship wrestling.

Let me hasten to point out that I don't personally give a flip whether there's a state lottery or not.

Well, I do, probably, but not because I want to play in a lottery.

I've never bought a lottery ticket, I don't plan to buy one in the future.

I do sometimes send in the cards for those lotteries we all get in the mail from time to time, the ones that Ed McMahon will personally notify us about if we win. But I never subscribe to the magazines.

To me, the only way to get any fun out of gambling is to throw dice or deal cards and watch the money change hands.

But, it seems to me, if the people of Virginia want a lottery, and some polls seem to indicate that they do, and since they're already playing lotteries in other states, and since it seems silly to let all that Virginia money build roads and do other good works in other states, it seems equally silly for the legislature to refuse to allow the people of Virginia to even record their opinion on the subject.

Thomas Jefferson would be appalled.

He had very little use for the idea that the people were not capable of making the decisions that affected their lives.

As to whether Virginians should be allowed to gamble, heck, we already do...

But we call it an election.

*September 1986*

I get a nostalgic fit every year about this time.
One part of me envies the kids and their chance to go out around the neighborhood and extort goodies from their neighbors, and another part of me feels a little sorry for them because things aren't as simple as they used to be.

In my youth, Halloween wasn't nearly as complicated as it is these days.

There were never any stories about some of the vile things that seem to crop up every year recently.

Halloween usually meant a party and some dunking for apples, and several cases of sniffles among the dunkers because the weather was always cool; and we always went home from the party in the same clothes we came in, but wet.

And the trick or treating was different.

Usually the treats were homemade candy or cookies, or taffy apples that could be depended on to be good and not tampered with in any way.

And the tricks played by the kids, especially in small towns and rural neighborhoods, were usually non-destructive.

I only remember participating in one really mean trick.

It was against the community crank.

We all called him Mister Charlie.

Mister Charlie never gave out any treats, he always ran us off.

So, one Halloween night, a bunch of us got some

rope and went over to Mister Charlie's house and tied the door to Mister Charlie's outhouse shut, after waiting in the dark for some time to be sure that Mister Charlie was in it.

Mister Charlie knew who did it and told our parents. But they didn't punish us too bad; they knew Mister Charlie was mean and had it coming — some even suspected that he voted for Thomas Dewey.

*October 1984*

A few days ago I was lamenting the fact that only about half of the folks in this country who could vote, if they wanted to, want to.

Well, I had a number of responses, mostly from folks who feel essentially the same as I, that voting is a right and a duty and that every citizen should exercise that right and perform that duty.

But, there was one fellow who wrote me a well thought out letter of disagreement.

It's his position that the Bill of Rights, freedom, justice, the rule of law, individual liberty, and the Constitution have been so eroded that it doesn't surprise him at all that many citizens refuse or neglect to vote.

And guess what brought about this total erosion of the American way of life?

Watergate...

That's right... Watergate didn't come out the way this writer thought it should, so in response, he's giving up on the whole shooting match.

Well.

I guess I can't get too upset about that.

Watergate didn't come out quite the way I thought it should either, but I plan to hang in there and I suspect a lot of others will, too.

The Constitution and the Bill of Rights have been transgressed many times, but that doesn't mean there's anything wrong with the Constitution and the Bill of Rights. It just means we sometimes get some less than perfect humans in the way of perfect justice.

But I don't know of any surer way to lose a war, or for that matter, a contest of any kind, than to retire from the field of combat.

The Constitution and Bill of Rights define what we should expect, indeed insist on, but there's nothing in there about free delivery.

*October 1984*

People often ask me what we raise on our farm at Elam, other than dogs, cats, and Cain on Saturday nights.

Well, not very much, really...

We have several fields where crops could probably be planted, but haven't been in quite some time.

Those fields now sport abundant crops of all sorts of grasses and weeds.

Then there's the meadows.

Alfalfa and fescue fight it out for supremacy on the meadows, and the fellow who cuts and bales whatever grows there usually prays for the alfalfa because it makes better hay, but he usually gets the fescue.

We have a couple of ancient apple trees.

One usually has apples, and the other one usually doesn't.

The one that does have apples, usually, also has a good sized hornet's nest, too; and you have no idea how the presence of a hornet's nest can diminish the desire for an apple.

Maybe it's because I have this peculiar talent...

If there is an apple on that tree with a hornet on the other side of it, that's the apple I will invariably pick.

About the only thing we have enough of for commercial exploitation at Elam is persimmons.

We have hundreds of persimmon trees and they always bear heavily, and I always try them at least eight times for the proper state of ripeness.

On each of those eight occasions, I go about for hours with a sort of semi-permanent pucker. But I have faith, I guess, since I keep on trying them and at the moment I can faithfully report that I have never tasted a persimmon, at any stage of ripeness, that doesn't produce a pucker.

Not a very good crop report, unless you count the dogs, and cats, and Cain on Saturday night.

*October 1984*

Here a few nights ago, I talked about the things that grow on our farm at Elam, and mentioned that the only bumper crop we ever have is persimmons and that that doesn't do me much good since I never seem to be able to pick persimmons at the right time and wind up with my lips incurably puckered for hours.

Well, the audience came through, as they always do.

Years ago, I had trouble with groundhogs eating my garden at Elam, and before long the advice from listeners came pouring in.

I now have the western hemisphere's greatest collection of groundhog lore; how to trap them, how to get them to move away, how to forecast weather with them, how to learn to love them, and how to cook them.

Listeners have also helped me with frozen pipes, the training of Irish setters, and politics.

So, it came as no surprise to me when the pertinent facts on persimmons started to trickle in.

Some hold that one must never eat persimmons before the first frost, that freezing eliminates the pucker factor and promotes the sweetness.

One persimmon expert says one must never pick a persimmon and eat it, but taste only fallen persimmons that sorta flatten out when they hit the ground.

I'm gonna test these theories this very year.

Anyway, the whole thing reminds me of a lovely passage in Lawrence Maddry's book, *Catcall and Pratfall on the Back Fence of Life.*

Lawrence tells of this small country church that found itself out of communion wine one Sunday and one of the parishioners went home for a quantity of persimmon beer for the service.

The beer, however, turned out to have been made with unripe persimmons.

They had to whistle the closing hymn.

*October 1984*

I have to apologize, I have been remiss...

A viewer reminded me today that I allowed the Columbus Day holiday to slip by this year without reviving the old argument as to whether it was Columbus or Leif Ericson who discovered America.

Well, I've revised my opinion on that since last year.

I believe it was actually a Russian who discovered America, and the information was filed away in the same department that keeps us in touch with the health of the current Soviet premier.

Joe Foulkes believes that the weather bureau discovered America while it was searching around Bermuda for whatever it was that was causing all those hurricanes.

Joe Foulkes, by the way, will be back from vacation soon and I plan to run my Russian theory by him while he's rested and can think clearly.

Anyway, Columbus Day was on Monday and I did miss it and I think it was because Congress was in session and I am not accustomed to seeing Congress in session on a holiday.

Congress was in session for a good reason, of course, trying to get some work done that should have been done at least two weeks before, but wasn't, and looks like it won't be until they agree on a budget, which doesn't seem likely as long as they can keep passing emergency legislation to cover the fact that there wouldn't be an emergency if they had done their work in a timely fashion in the first place...

The current emergency, at last report, was scheduled to end tomorrow (10/10/84), at which time our Congress is expected to have a new emergency ready for distribution.

Trying to keep track of all that — no wonder I missed Columbus Day.

*October 1984*

Well, I watched the debate last night (10/21/84) and I longed deep in my soul that Will Rogers could have been there to watch it with me, and perhaps make some sense of it afterward.

About the most powerful thing I heard said all night was in reference to the difference of opinion between Mister Reagan and Mister Mondale on whether to give defensive technology to the Russians, someday, if such is ever developed, that could render nuclear weapons obsolete.

The president said he'd give that technology to the Russians.

Senator and former Vice President Mondale said he wouldn't.

David Brinkley made the only sensible and pertinent comment afterward, though, when he observed rightly that there's nothing to give just yet.

Anyway, it finally sank in on me during this debate just what it is about debates that bothers me, aside from the fact that these election year things we've witnessed haven't really been debates in the formal sense of the word...

It's the reporters.

Where is it written that reporters should get to ask all the questions?

Sure, reporters make their living asking questions, but so do lawyers; and I haven't noticed any groundswell to allow lawyers to set the agenda for these debates.

If I could make the rules, I'd let the questions on the economy be asked by a grocer, or a barber, or an insurance salesman, somebody who knows whether people have any money left after taxes, and what they do with it.

Foreign policy questions should be handled by soldiers, sailors, or marines, somebody who may have to do the work if a president turned out to be wrong.

The judging, well, I'd hire a plumber to tell us whether the arguments hold water.

*October 1984*

In spite of my reluctance to believe in polls, or rather to believe that polls serve any very useful purpose, I do read them.

For one thing, I want to know how the questions were phrased that led to the figures.

For example, did they ask whom do you love the

most, or whom do you hate the least?

Anyway, the important poll is the one that will be taken on November 6.

I'll pay attention to that one.

I paid attention to a similar one that was held four years ago, almost. And that one came to my attention again today, and it was disturbing.

In that poll four years ago, only fifty-three percent of those eligible to vote bothered to do so.

Mind you, that's not fifty-three percent of those who could have voted if they'd been registered, that's fifty-three percent of those who were registered.

Imagine that, just to give away a right that had to be bought at the price this country has been paying for two hundred years.

Just to give away a right that people in other countries are dying for right now...

The strange thing about it is — and this isn't statistics, just personal experience — there's hardly anyone among us who doesn't complain about government at some level at least once a week and yet nearly half of us are willing to allow somebody else to decide the makeup of that government for years to come.

The Russians do better than that and they don't even have two parties.

I guess it shows what a great and abiding faith we have that somebody will do the right thing.

But let's face it, there's going to be a government, whether we help pick it or not.

*October 1984*

In times past, on rare occasions, I have used this space to talk about the joys and trials of owning an Irish setter.

Our Irish setter, Murphy, came to us several years ago by way of the Virginia Beach S.P.C.A.

The way it happened, one of our photographers was filming a story about the S.P.C.A., and during the course of that assignment he took pictures of Murphy, and those pictures got on the air. And my wife, who has a soft spot for Irish setters, but had at that time no knowledge of Irish setters beyond the fact that they are beautiful...

Are you following this?

Anyway, my wife saw those pictures of Murphy and decided that our farm at Elam needed an Irish setter and that Murphy was the very Irish setter our farm at Elam needed, and therefore that we should begin adoption proceedings immediately.

And we did.

And have spent the past four years trying to teach Murphy not to chase cars, ducks, cats, and trying to make an honest dog of him.

He doesn't chase cars, cats, or ducks any more, but he's still a thief.

I sure hope you're following all this.

Anyway, you'd think, with that experience behind me, I would know that letting my wife get into the vicinity of S.P.C.A. shelters where Irish setters may be available, is not a good idea.

Well, I do know that.

But she went out to the S.P.C.A. in Virginia Beach the other day, anyway...

Not to get an Irish setter, of course. We already have an Irish setter, but I think you probably know what's coming next.

That's right. The good folks at the Virginia Beach S.P.C.A. had an Irish setter.

We pick her up Friday.

*October 1984*

Years ago our Congress decided that the fiscal year needed changing.

It started in July if I remember correctly, but it could have been June, or some other month.

I do remember that the old fiscal year started months earlier than it does now.

Personally, I have always felt that starting the year in January made sense; but that was a problem for Congress, since if they started the year in January the way everybody else does, it would make it more troublesome to cloud the issues. And if there's one thing Congress can't stand, it's an unclouded issue.

Anyway, back when the fiscal year started several months earlier than it does now, it was decided in the halls of Congress that the fiscal year was starting much too early, and that it didn't give them time to settle on a national budget.

So, they set the beginning of the fiscal year back to October 1, or thereabouts, I'm not sure...

I only know that they treat the new beginning of the fiscal year in much the same manner as they treated the old one — as a time to report to the American people that they haven't had time to settle the budget; and then they want us to regard them as some sort of heroes when they sit up all night arguing about whose fault it is.

I know it's complicated to make a budget for something as big as the United States; but they asked for the job, didn't they? And think about this, did you ever hear anybody campaigning for the House or the Senate who didn't tell you he, or she, knew how to do the job?

A lot of us get calendars from our congressmen and senators, especially during an election year, calendars that start a year in January.

I think we need to send *them* one, and hire somebody to teach them how to read it.

*October 1984*

Well, I went ahead and did it...

I had planned to avoid it and usually when I plan to avoid something, I manage to succeed in avoiding it; but as the evening wore on last night, and the presidential debate came closer and closer, I weakened and finally gave in. And sure enough, I sat there in my own living room and watched Walter Mondale and Ronald Reagan debate.

At least that's what I intended to watch.

I'm not sure what I saw, but it wasn't what Miss Priddy would have called a debate.

Miss Priddy was my high school English teacher.

She was also my literature teacher.

She was also my debating coach.

It was a small high school.

Anyway, I wasn't much of a debater in high school, but I did pay attention when Miss Priddy had something to say.

If you went to Russellville High, and wanted to graduate while you were still young and single, it was a good idea to pay attention when Miss Priddy had something to say.

Miss Priddy is gone to her reward now and was blessedly spared the spectacle of that debate last night (10/7/84). And that's probably just as well, she would have had a fit.

Their math, what there was of it, was awful; their arguments were weak; they changed the subject whenever it suited them.

I can hear Miss Priddy now, "Wally, stop that meandering around all over a subject and make one good solid point," and, "Ronnie, stop saying uh-uh-uh constantly, if you'd studied for this you'd be able to use your time for argument"...

I don't know which one won the most votes, but I know for sure that both would have failed Miss Priddy's class. They'd have been lucky if she didn't hold them back and make them go to summer school.

October 1984

Surely there's somebody out there who can help me with this problem.

It's like this.

A few weeks ago, there was an article in the Wall Street Journal about hot dogs.

Well, actually, it wasn't about hot dogs; it was about that strange set of facts surrounding hot dogs that most of us have probably wondered about, but never thought to ask about.

The article opened with a question.

Why is it, the article asked, that the people who package hot dogs always put ten of them in a package; but, the people who package hot dog buns always put either eight or twelve buns to a package.

The way it works out, if you buy a package of hot dogs and a package of hot dog buns, you always wind up either two buns short, or two buns to the surplus side.

I did some study on the problem once and discovered that there is probably no way to make the buns and hot dogs come out even without buying eight packages of ten hot dogs, and ten packages of eight hot dog buns, or five packages of twelve hot dog buns and six packages of ten hot dogs.

I have never cared enough for hot dogs to try this experiment at home, so it remains in the realm of theory, but you're welcome to try if you care to.

My problem is this. I read only the question and was interrupted before I got to the part of the article that would have, I am sure, cleared up this mystery once and for all. And while I was off doing whatever it was that needed doing on that occasion, somebody swiped my copy of the Wall Street Journal.

Maybe somebody read it and can fill me in.

I asked my wife, and she said she didn't bother to read the article; said when you have an Irish setter, extra buns or hot dogs are no problem.

*October 1984*

I've watched a lot of political campaigns, and I think I'm getting the hang of how one goes about running for office.

I have no plans at present to run for office, but a lot of people down through the years who have never run for political office have decided to run for political office, and some of them get elected...

So, on the off-chance I may someday find myself out of work and in need of something to do that keeps me inside and out of the wet, I have been watching people who run for political office and trying to determine how it is that they do whatever it is that they do to get elected.

Since I'm not running in the current election, I'm willing to share this knowledge with you...

For one thing, if you're elected to high political office, it may be necessary to raise taxes to fund the promises you make; so it's necessary to discuss this with the voters, who unfortunately, may also be the same folks whose taxes will have to be raised.

There are two approaches to this problem.

There's the Reagan approach whereby you simply deny it.

That's right. Tell those voters that you don't intend to raise taxes. Period. Unless it becomes necessary.

Then, there's the Mondale approach whereby you go before an audience of voters and courageously admit that you do intend to raise taxes, somebody else's taxes.

Either of these approaches is effective, and about as straightforward as we require our politicians to be.

In future seminars I will discuss foolproof methods of running for Congress on a foolproof platform of cutting government waste and foolish spending, in somebody else's district...

*October 1984*


Alligators have never been among my favorite animals.

Don't get me wrong. I love animals, in general, and dogs and cats in particular, but I've just never felt moved to go out of my way to friendly up to alligators.

Even a few years ago when alligators were supposedly an endangered species, I didn't sit up nights worrying about alligators.

Possibly because I never really believed they were endangered and possibly because I ran over one once back in the sixties in Louisiana.

It didn't hurt the gator, but it put my car on the sick list about two hundred dollars worth, as near as I can remember.

I didn't mean to run over that gator...

It's just that when you come around a curve and find a gator taking up half the road, and taking his half in the middle, there's nothing much you can do about it.

In that part of Louisiana everything that wasn't road was swamp, so I hit him rather than elect to go into the swamp and possibly disturb his brothers and uncles — you get the picture.

Anyway, I read in the Washington Post yesterday that

they're prosecuting a man in Alabama, the Interior Department is, for cooking some of an alligator that was killed when it endangered some children.

Today I read in the Wall Street Journal that some parts of Texas are eyeball deep in alligators.

Hungry ones, that eat bird dogs, calves, anything handy...

I just wonder if the U.S. District Court in Alabama couldn't reduce its workload a bit by arranging to get some of the Texas alligators transferred to Alabama, where they seem to be short of alligators.

Of course I'm not in government, I don't know — it's just a thought.

*October 1985*

I don't always agree with the editorials in the New York Times. But I read them, almost every day, in the belief that I might occasionally learn something.

And yesterday I did.

Learn something.

And I'm happy to report to you that you need have no fear of being devastated by killer bees anytime soon. Our government has the money to fight that invasion, if and when it comes.

A million dollars is approved by both Houses of Congress in the new appropriations bill, the one for 1987, which started last Wednesday according to Congress.

The Congress has committed you and me to come up with one half trillion dollars for 1987, because killer bees are not all they're worried about.

In amongst all the things that we need to be worried about, and spend the money for, or against as the case may be, there are a few items that you and I might consider taking out of the budget if we had our druthers.

But, in the Congress, when you want a few billion for a project that's happening in your district, and fiscal restraint appears to be threatening, you get together with some other lawmakers who want something special in their district and take turns giving each other what you want.

For example, war reparations.

How's that? I thought we had just about paid up for World War II, and Korea, and Vietnam, and Grenada.

No, we're talking the Civil War, or if you prefer, the War between the States, or if you prefer, the War of Northern Aggression; anyway, the Great Unpleasantness.

Senator Matthias of Maryland got two hundred thousand dollars appropriated to reimburse Frederick, Maryland, for ransom it paid to keep the Confederate Army from burning it.

Boy, some people sure can hold a grudge.

But, if such a theft doesn't frost you, you're thicker skinned and more lightly taxed than I am.

October 1986

I believe it was Will Rogers who said he didn't care what they said about him in the papers as long as they spelled his name right.

I don't know.

It could have been Franklin Roosevelt or Frank Sinatra.

Anyway.

There's an old belief among people who are in the public eye that it's best not to answer the scurrilous attacks sometimes made upon one in the press.

And I've followed that advice.

Mostly.

When a local columnist suggested that I had made up a place called Elam in Virginia so I would have something to write about when I had nothing to write about, I let that pass.

I've been reasonable, I think.

But, a copy of the latest Portfolio Magazine has come into my hands and it contains an item that I must, in all good conscience, answer.

In the "Overheard" column on page five, under the heading "Hot Tip," Portfolio says, and I quote - "We heard that Jim Kincaid does not write his folksy blurbs that he delivers with good style on WVEC-TV, but gets them from the New York firm of Jacobs, Bozell, and Cancroft, the folks who represent the fellows who do the Bartles and Jaymes commercials."

Unquote.

Boy does that hurt.

Comparing the deathless prose and occasional lofty poetry that flows from my mind, through my fingertips, and onto paper as the work of people who write wine cooler commercials, that hurts.

I can accept the part about delivering them with style — that's good accurate journalism.

Let me assure you that I write my own material and take full responsibility for it...

And I thank you for your support.

*October 1986*

You can always tell when the World's Series is being played in this country.

That's because people who do not ordinarily watch baseball at all during the regular season, watch baseball with greater interest and see things that regular watchers of baseball don't notice.

How do I know this?

Because they call me and write to me and say things

to me on the street, and because I'm that sort of baseball fan.

I guess I figure that when something comes down to just two teams out of several dozen, that an opportunity to watch them do whatever it is that they do will also be an opportunity to see the best of the best at whatever that is.

But it's probably not a good idea to watch baseball on a part time basis.

Mainly because of what I mentioned before, we seldom-if-at-all types notice things that the truly faithful do not see.

Like the result of the influence on the salivary glands of chewing tobacco.

In my mother's house you not only didn't do such a thing in the sight or hearing of civilized people, you didn't discuss it either.

But ballplayers do it all the time.

Like I say, I led a sheltered life where chewing tobacco was concerned, though I did try it — once — before I learned that that habit my mother so detested was absolutely essential to the art of chewing tobacco.

I gave up chewing tobacco that same day, forever.

I guess I have always wondered why anyone would take a habit that makes a fellow wonder how soon he may be allowed to die and get it over with.

So I asked a ballplayer once why he chewed tobacco.

"Image, son," he said, "image."

*October 1986*


Both on the air and in print lately there's been a lot of weeping and wailing and gnashing of teeth about negative political advertising.

It seems that just about everybody, with the possible

exception of the politicians and their ad agencies, feels negative advertising is a bad thing.

Well, I agree, but there's certainly nothing new about it.

Politicians have been saying rotten things about each other since the beginnings of recorded history and I'll give you odds that it was going on before that.

It probably began when our cave dwelling ancestors discovered that a battle to the death with stone axes made entering public service a risky business at best, and decided that merely impeaching one another's character was less bloody and more fun in the long run.

Thus was the art of politics born and it hasn't changed much since.

Having one politician go on television and accuse his opponent of being personally responsible for everything that's gone wrong in the past two, or four, or six years is not different in the essentials from Oog standing in the cave door and shouting that it was Moog that let that saber-toothed tiger in, here a moon or so ago; and who wants to live under an administration like that?

The technology is somewhat advanced but the spirit is quite the same.

What can we do about it?

Probably not much.

Unless, unless we make it clear at the ballot box that we wish the gentlemen and ladies who want to be on our payroll to *be* gentlemen and ladies, and to ask for the job on their own merits, and not the demerits of somebody else.

It's a radical idea, but it could work.

*October 1986*


Sam Taylor believes we're going to have a late winter, but when it does get here, it'll be a doozy.

Sam predicts bone chilling cold for January and February and a blizzard in March.

Sam, by the way, is a retired newspaper reporter from Lancaster, Pennsylvania, and as such I would be inclined to doubt him if it were not for the source of his information.

Sam gets his weather directly from the woolly bear caterpillar which has been commissioned to do weather in this country since colonial times.

Sam says his reading of woolly bears in his part of the country leads him to believe we're in for a hard winter.

The woolly bears of Elam agree.

If you base the severity of the winter on the width of the dark stripe of the woolly bear, that is.

If you go the other way, and figure the light stripe foretells severe weather, then we're likely to have a mild winter.

But I'm a dark stripe man and I think it'll be a cold winter.

I've also noticed another natural phenomenon that the scientists have missed.

That being that the winter will always last at least two weeks longer than my woodpile at Elam.

When you heat with wood you notice things like that.

The Farmer's Almanac has a fellow who uses sunspots to predict long range weather and I've noticed that his predictions are never wrong.

They're not necessarily right, either, just written in such a way that they'll pretty much fit whatever happens.

Sorta like a political speech.

Nossir, gimme woolly bears and I'll give you a prediction that's at least as good as a political promise. And, like a politician, I'll fess up next spring if I turn out to be right.

*October 1986*

*Woolly bears tell you about winter.*

I realize I look extraordinarily youthful and well-preserved for a fellow past the half century mark, folks, but I don't want you to get the idea that I haven't faced some hardships in life.

Some unusually severe hardships.

For example, I had the misfortune to grow up in a family where two of my mother's three sons were members of the United States Marine Corps, and the other was drafted into the Army.

I happened to be the other one.

If you've never had an accident like that you have no idea how difficult it is to be the non-Marine.

No matter how extreme the hardship I faced in the army, one of my brothers would always chime in with sufferings much worse, and then he would be topped by the other, older brother, who was in the Corps first, when it was really rough to be a Marine.

You probably get the picture.

If I had made a fifty-mile forced march before breakfast with full pack and combat gear, my brothers would come back with the Marine equivalent, a three-day survival ordeal in the dense jungle with nothing but a pocket knife and a recent copy of Leatherneck Magazine.

Rough guys, those Marines, and they never let a fellow forget it.

Well.

I don't know what's going to happen when my brothers find out what I found out today.

The Marine Corps has abolished K.P.

It takes too much time away from a Marine's opportunity to do the things he joined the Marine Corps for in the first place.

From now on, the cleaning and scraping, the hardships of the kitchen police, will be in the hands of civilians.

It'll break my brothers' hearts.
Think I'll call them tonight.

*October 1986*

I got into a conversation the other day with a caller who was mourning the mass of misinformation the various candidates in the upcoming election have been spreading about one another.

He wanted to know what I was going to do about it.

I told him I probably wasn't going to do anything about it and the government probably won't either.

But it is a problem.

And it stems from the fact that we don't have any very effective laws in this country on the telling of half truths.

If you're running for office and want to buy an ad, or a television commercial, and use that commercial to mislead the public about your opponent through the clever use of half truth, there's nothing much that a newspaper or a television station can do about that.

There's been a lot of it this year, at all levels, but there's nothing new about that; it's just one of those imperfections of a free democracy that we'll probably have to live with.

The cure, unfortunately, would be to test political statements thoroughly, like we test drugs and foods, and try to eliminate all those that are in any way harmful, or untrue in the case of political statements.

In which case, of course, the entire political process in this country would fall silent.

And that, of course, would be unconstitutional.

What we can do about it is seek out all the information we can; and it's usually available if we look, and decide for ourselves and record that decision in a voting booth next Tuesday.

It won't eliminate half truth by any means, but it will let them know which half we believe.

*November 1984*

Campaign statements have always fascinated me.

I often wonder how many people are more impressed by how a politician says something than by what he says, or perhaps, more inclined to believe a politician based on his political party than his political principles.

Thought I'd try a little trivia quiz with you today, this being election day and all, and you've probably already voted, if you planned to vote at all.

Try to fit these following statements with the candidate and the party:

One... "We have always known that heedless self-interest was bad morals, now we know that it is bad economics."

Two... "The test of our progress is not whether we add more to the abundance of those who have much, it is whether we provide enough for those who have too little."

Three... "I have said this before, but I shall say it again and again and again — your boys are not going to be sent into any foreign wars."

Four... "We are moving forward to greater security for the average man than he has ever known before in the history of America."

Five... "I see one third of a nation ill housed, ill clad, ill nourished."

Six... "The only sure bulwark of continuing liberty is a government strong enough to protect the interests of the people."

Seven... and last in the quiz. "The Soviet Union, as everyone knows, is run by a dictatorship as absolute as any other dictatorship in the world."

Sorta spans the political spectrum, doesn't it.

Score yourself a hundred if you identified all the quotes correctly, with one name, Franklin Delano Roosevelt.

*November 1984*

Well, this time tomorrow it'll be mostly over and we'll spend the balance of the evening learning what the voters said, and no doubt, having a lot of experts telling us why they said it, and even more experts trying to figure out just what they meant by it.

There will be the quadrennial fuss about exit polling and whether the folks in California decided for or against a candidate's merits based on what the voters back east did earlier.

Then there's all those earlier polls, the ones showing the president way ahead of Mondale.

Some political analysts will blame them for whatever happens.

I don't worry too much about that since I believe that folks who really feel they have a stake in America will vote, and vote for the best set of candidates in their opinion, no matter whether they feel confident or hopeless.

Sure, some folks will decide not to take the trouble because they figure their guy is a lost cause.

In the final analysis, it's going to be the folks who do vote who will decide the tenancy at the White House for the next four years.

I figure it this way.

If the Soviet Union can turn out over ninety percent of its people to vote for no choice at all in a system that doesn't work, we should feel an obligation to record our choice in a system that does.

See you at the polls.

*November 1984*

Since the election a few days ago, I've been reading a lot about what it means to, and more to the point, what the election said about, the American people.

I've agreed with some of what I've read, disagreed with some of it, been elated, and saddened.

I guess that's one of the nice things about living in a country such as ours; there's room for all shades of opinion.

But one note that's been repeated several times bothers me a bit; that being the charge that the American people voted their self-interest — as though that's a bad thing.

Well, what free people given the opportunity to make the choices they consider closest to their own feelings, would vote against those choices?

I don't think the American people are selfish.

Consider the case of Baby Fae. Didn't we all feel a sense of loss when she lost her fight?

The Ethiopian famine... Americans are responding from their hearts and pocketbooks. And if anyone cared to take a poll among those responding, I daresay he wouldn't be able to make out any meaningful political orientation one way or the other.

How would you like to sit down and make a list of those organizations in this country that make it their full time business to help others, and do it with the voluntary time, energy, and funds of our fellow citizens.

Selfish?

I'll need more than the word of a few columnists to convince me.

Maybe this renewal of the American spirit really has nothing to do with politics at all.

Maybe it has to do with the facts that are apparent the minute we examine the evidence.

As a nation, we're a pretty good bunch.

*November 1984*


The story was in the Washington Post today (11/9/84) and it should have headlined this and all other news broadcasts and newspapers in this area.

Big news.

The Navy is returning to Navy talk.

Bureaucratese is no longer required.

Kitchens which were always galleys until some civilian bureaucrat got hold of them in the seventies, will become galleys once again.

And, if you joined the Navy since the seventies, you will no longer be required to eat in enlisted dining facilities or officer dining facilities, you can get just as good a meal on the mess deck and you'll get there by way of hatches and passageways instead of doors and halls.

Navy Secretary John Lehman says so.

Rejoice salts... those stairways have become ladders again and they lead topside, and those walls are bulkheads.

Secretary Lehman says this new, modern terminology that turns barracks into unaccompanied enlisted personnel housing has been sticking in his craw for some time.

Says most sailors never learned to talk that way anyway, but had to write that way on official documents, which made for a lot of confusion and the gradual elimination of the Navy's very colorful language.

So, he's apparently decided to bring the old colorful Navy language topside again and deep six bureaucratese.

At least the part that can be used in mixed company...

The part that can't was never in danger anyway.

*November 1984*

Yesterday (11/11/84) was Veterans' Day, of course, and so is today officially; and though I usually frown on the practice of moving holidays around just so they can occur on a Monday, I approve in this case.

In fact, one store in Washington has declared this to be Veterans' Week.

That's just so they can extend their Veterans' Day sale I guess, but it isn't a bad idea.

A week to set aside and thank those who have put on their nation's uniform would still be a bit on the short side.

We should thank them every day.

But, isn't it nice that we seem, finally, to be sorting out our feelings about Vietnam.

Sure, there are still plenty of folks who will continue to believe that our involvement there was wrong; and those who will continue to believe that we had no business leaving before the job was done; and people who will continue to hold various shades of many other opinions.

But, as to the honor due those who risked their lives, or their mental and physical health in their country's service, the opinions no longer seem to be so sharply divided.

The political and sociological and historical complexities are subject to debate; and they will be.

But the meeting of an armed enemy in the field has little to do with any of that.

Courage, sense of duty, patriotism, that's not all of it either.

You had to be there.

And — they were there.

And for that, we owe them an undebatable and undying gratitude.

*November 1984*


I bet you thought the political season was over.

It's not.

Now that the election is over, the new season begins, headed toward a sort of national half time ceremony two years from now, and another presidential election four years down the road.

The Super Bowl of politics.

And to carry the football analogy further, the coaches and managers of the major teams will begin almost immediately to look at the game film and try to figure out what worked, and what didn't, and use that information to build a winning strategy for next time.

Of course, politics isn't really like football at all.

They have rules in football.

Oh, they have rules in politics, too, sorta, but you can get caught breaking them and still win the game if the officials, in this case the voting public, like you better.

But for now, the experts are gearing up to give us the specific reasons the election came out the way it did.

They'll cite the economic climate, the nuclear issue, the social welfare issue, inflation, taxes, housing costs, military spending, the debates, whether it was time for a woman on the ticket, and they'll all be right and wrong to one degree or another...

Some of us pick a candidate on the issues, some on the way he cuts his hair.

Whatever, the votes are in; the decision has been made and the new campaign is underway.

I don't know who'll run. But I'd bet you can expect to hear a lot from Vice President Bush and Gary Hart in the near future; and when Congress reconvenes, a lot about taxes, this time with the Democrats against them.

And, it wouldn't surprise me if the president didn't meet with a Soviet premier before long, if they can get one who isn't prone to headcolds.

*November 1984*

I can't wait to see what that jury in California will decide about cigarettes.

The way it works — the plaintiffs in this case are claiming that the man who died — and thus brought the case about — was addicted to cigarettes and couldn't stop smoking, even after he developed some of the dread diseases that, we all know by now, or should, are connected to cigarette smoking.

One of the lawyers on that side of the case is Melvin Belli.

I saw him work a trial once a long time ago, and I feel a little sorry for the other side since Melvin Belli has a habit of convincing juries that his beliefs are hard facts, not to be denied by any sensible, right-thinking person.

The issue seems to be whether cigarettes are more than just a habit, but indeed a true addiction like heroin, or any number of other drugs. And Melvin Belli now believes this to be the case.

The defendants, a tobacco company, say cigarettes are just a habit and can be put aside by anyone who seriously wants to.

I know that to be true.

I used to smoke cigarettes myself, but I stopped smoking cigarettes several months ago and went to full time pipe smoking.

I was clearly not an addict...

It took me less than thirty years to give up cigarettes, and I expect, if I live another thirty years, to be able to put aside the pipe just as easily.

Lawyer Belli said last night on Nightline that he would be willing to have smokers on that jury, since smokers would know that he's right, that it is an addiction.

I think the outcome will depend on how long the trial sessions last; any smoker can tell you that during the first hour or so without a smoke it's just a habit — after that, you know jolly well it's an addiction.

*November 1985*


I don't have too many things in common with presidents.

For instance, I'm hardly ever invited to summit conferences and things like that.

But, I believe President Reagan and I could sit down and talk about dogs and get along fine.

Maybe you've heard that Lucky, the President's White House dog, is being retired to the ranch in California.

I could have predicted that would happen.

I've seen pictures of the President, and of Mrs.

Reagan, leading Lucky - or, more accurately - I've seen pictures of Lucky leading the Reagans...

Having seen those scenes, I developed an understanding of the Reagans that goes far deeper than party politics.

The Reagans, in sum, have a Murphy on their hands.

Murphy is my Irish setter.

Murphy was acquired when all I knew about Irish setters was summed up in whiskey ads in magazines that showed Irish setters lying quietly and regally beside their masters' chairs.

The ads lie...

I don't know how they got an Irish setter to lie quietly and regally long enough to take a picture, but Irish setters don't do that.

They may eat the chair, but they don't lie quietly and regally beside it.

I suspect that the Reagans got Lucky on the basis of the same sort of misinformation.

Once thoroughly acquainted with the real facts about big friendly dogs, the Reagans decided wisely that Lucky needed room to run.

I decided that about Murphy the day we got him and took him to our farm at Elam.

Now Lucky gets to be a country dog and the President can spend his time constructively — fighting with Tip O'Neal.

November 1985

This new study on coffee, that's trouble folks, pure and simple — trouble.

You've heard by now, five cups of coffee a day and you're a candidate for heart problems.

Three times more likely, according to the Johns Hopkins Medical School, to have heart problems than people who don't drink coffee at all.

Sometimes I think you just can't win no matter what.

Here I've stopped smoking cigarettes.

I've cut down on my salt intake.

I exercise every day.

I've moderated my intake of red meat and other things that might contain cholesterol.

I have become, while not exactly a teetotaler, a very modest and moderate consumer of alcoholic beverages.

The Jack Daniels folks don't send me presents any more.

I even vote conservative.

And now, now, after I've sacrificed practically everything but that, I find I have to either give up or feel guilty about coffee.

Five cups a day.

Heck, I drink that before breakfast and I always have coffe with breakfast. And after breakfast, I get down to some serious coffee drinking.

I can see it now. A few years down the road those of us who drink coffee will have to sit in the back of the plane. And they'll have coffee or no-coffee sections in restaurants. And those of us who brazen it out, and drink coffee anyway, will have to suffer the icy stares and rude comments of the non-coffee drinkers among us. We'll be shunned and if we don't die of heart trouble, we'll die of loneliness.

If being good and healthy is all that troublesome, I wonder why folks think it's so important.

*November 1985*

Thanksgiving Day is a lot of things to a lot of people. Throughout the day, we'll read and hear about what this one or that one has to be thankful for, and how it all got started.

And, there'll be the old argument renewed about whether the first Thanksgiving was celebrated in Virginia or in Massachusetts.

I'm a Virginia sympathizer myself, but that could be because I live in Virginia.

There is something to be said for the Massachusetts Thanksgiving though, in terms of hardiness, because I believe that anyone who finds himself in Massachusetts in late November and can still be thankful has a great capacity for thankfulness, and should be respected for it.

We're all thankful, of course, or should be, to live in a free country.

But I think we should be especially thankful to some of our forefathers and foremothers for things they did for us that are not overly obvious and thus don't get talked about enough in history books.

The Plymouth pilgrims, for example...

They tried communism.

They called the first Thanksgiving after they switched over to private enterprise.

Communism, it seems, didn't produce much of anything to be thankful for except mutual starvation.

Then there's Ben Franklin.

Our forefathers and foremothers took a lot of his advice to our very great benefit, but when he suggested making the turkey our national bird, they nixed that idea.

After all, even if eagles are morally inferior to the turkey, as Franklin thought they were, they still look good on coins and flagpoles; and that leaves turkeys for eating which you just can't do with your national bird. Our forebears knew you can't trust a vegetarian to pick your national bird.

*November 1985*

A fellow called me today to say that he was somewhat confused.

When he told me what he was confused about, I had to agree that he had every right to be confused. And that, if it was any help, I was just as confused as he was.

What he doesn't understand is what all the fuss is about with regard to this upcoming highly secret shuttle mission that turns out to be not very secret after all.

It seems to him, and to me as well, that it is unwise if you're going to try to keep a secret to announce to the world that you're about to do something but you won't say what it is.

That just naturally arouses the curiosity, especially of Americans who are curious by nature, and inclined by that same nature to go out of their way to find out about anything that anybody tells them they won't tell them about.

When the Pentagon announced that we could not know what that upcoming shuttle mission was all about, and furthermore that we could not even speculate about it, that immediately spawned a search for knowledge on the subject, and a veritable waterfall of speculation about whatever it might be that the Pentagon doesn't want us to either know or speculate about.

The Pentagon even made some generals and such available not to reveal details on talk shows and such.

Well, I don't have any factual details, but I think it has something to do with keeping an eye on the Russians.

If they invade us successfully sometime down the

road, they would then have to occupy us, govern us, and administrate us...

If our Government can't do that, neither can theirs.

*December 1984*

With the approach of Christmas this year, as every year, the newspapers and magazines and radio and television shows are filled to overflowing with suggestions as to what to give for Christmas.

But nowhere in the media, this year or any other year, have I ever seen any suggestions that really do husbands any good.

Oh sure, there are all sorts of ads telling the beleaguered husband what his wife will like for Christmas, but wives quite often tell husbands that anyway.

What the average husband really needs to know this time of year is how to keep his wife from finding out what it is that he's giving her for Christmas.

I have worried about this problem for years, have come up with several theories on how to go about it and have been wrong every time.

For example, the old "put it in a package that doesn't look anything like there would be one of those in it"...

Don't do it guys, it never works.

I once gave my wife a watch wrapped in a shoebox and weighted with bricks.

She didn't lift, shake, measure, or listen to that package, but told me two days before Christmas that she could hardly wait to wear her new watch.

And don't give hints. No matter what. Wives have minds like computers and can translate the most harmless information into facts. Buy 'em a cat and tell them only that it's not an elephant — and they know unerringly that it's a cat.

But there may be hope.

I have employed a new method this year, and so far it's working.

I merely answer yes to any question she asks me on one day, and then no to any question the following day.

And smile, always smile, it drives 'em crazy.

*December 1984*

There has been considerable excitement in the Kincaid household for the past few days as we get ready for a Christmas vacation at Elam.

My wife and daughter appear to be ready.

I'm not so sure about their husband and father.

As many Christmases as I have had to practice on, I do not recall ever being ready.

But it does look pretty good this year.

I have avoided the battery problem by carefully avoiding to buy anything that runs on batteries.

The Christmas light strands will be tangled as usual, but I have three days to untangle them.

I have spare bulbs and some of my spares may even fit — that will be a first.

I have film for the camera, the flash unit is fully charged.

Wandering around on the land in recent weekends, I have spotted at least a few young pines that may fall within the framework of what my wife and daughter feel a Christmas tree should be.

Joe Foulkes has given me a private weather forecast that seems to promise that my pipes won't freeze on Christmas Day like they did last year.

I have, so far, successfully kept both wife and daughter from finding out what I'm giving them for Christmas, and if I make it till Christmas Eve, that will be another first.

So, on the whole, it looks like it will be a fine Christmas at our house — and I heartily wish the same for you and yours.

*December 1984*

I was mightily impressed by the news that the Congress of the United States is about to do something it rarely ever does.

Congress is going to work this weekend.

That's right.

Congress is going to remain in session right through the weekend to see if it can't head off another crisis.

I think they'll get the job done, they always do, since this is a crisis they have several times a year.

The government is about to run out of money again.

Now, the sarcastic among us might very well point out that the government has been out of money for some time, but that's not exactly so.

When you and I run out of money it's quite a different matter. We generally have to wait until we get some more, by working for it or inheriting it, or something. But the Congress merely has to authorize some more money.

The way I understand it, the congressional method works something like this.

You have a credit card and you spend more money on that credit card than you can afford to pay back in payments, so you can take another credit card to make the payments on that first credit card, and so on, and so on, until somebody catches you and insists that you pay his bill with real money.

The difference is, if you and I do that, we're bound to run into some troublemaker who wants real money in fairly short order.

What happens next is generally called bankruptcy.

When Congress does it, it's called deficit spending.

Somehow I wish they'd go home for the weekend, they get things fouled up enough during a regular week.

*December 1985*

Tragedy has a habit, it seems, of showing up at the wrong time.

When that chartered jet crashed the other day and took the lives of some of this country's finest young men, the pain was heightened by the fact that it's so near Christmas and these fellows were on their way home because it was nearing Christmas.

President Reagan was right when he said at the memorial service that there's nothing anyone can say to lessen the pain, especially for the loved ones of the men who died.

But I learned of one young woman who dealt with her grief and pain in a particularly noble and courageous way.

I won't tell you her name but I will tell you she was waiting for that flight to bring home her husband of six months.

They had spent only a month of that time together.

Not surprisingly, she had some gifts for her returning hero and plans for a happy Christmas.

But when that happy anticipation was turned suddenly to shock and grief, maybe even anger — it would be understandable — she took those gifts back to the store and got her money back.

Then, and this is what makes her story so special, she marched straight to an angel tree in the shopping mall, where the names of needy children are hung, and chose two angels. Then used her refunds to buy gifts for the children whose names and clothing sizes were listed on the angels she chose, thus turning her tragedy into warmth and joy for someone, someone she doesn't even know.

There's a lesson in there for those of us who have everything going our way - and I don't think I need to tell you what it is.

*December 1985*

I believe I'd like to hear the whole story on the Iran arms deal just about as much as anybody.

In fact, I'd like to hear the whole truth just as soon as possible so we could get back to at least some of the other business around the world.

But, I predicted a few days ago that this particular scandal will last at least two years.

That's about how long it is till the next presidential election.

And, for those two years, we're going to hear the same questions asked over and over again, then the results of a poll as to what percentage of the American people believe the latest set of answers.

But, of all the questions we'll hear asked, and re-asked in coming months, the silliest of all has to be, why didn't the President inform Congress of this change in policy in a timely fashion?

Why...?

The president can't answer that question, at least diplomatically, but I can.

The reason the president didn't inform the Congress of what he was doing behind the scenes is because informing Congress, even in secret closed sessions, is the same as printing the information on the front page of the Washington Post.

If you don't believe me, pick up a copy of today's Post (12/3/86).

On the front page a detailed story of a closed meeting of the Senate Intelligence Committee meeting yesterday in which Senate sources revealed all, who said what, who testified, how unhappy the senators were that all the questions were not answered.

What the Washington Post fails to point out is the fact that such leakage of closed session testimony by a senator, or a staffer, is illegal, a violation of federal law, Senate rules, and common sense.

It's also why the President didn't confide in Congress in timely fashion.

*December 1986*


My daughter and her boyfriend have made it tough on me this Christmas.

They found a perfect Christmas tree for our digs here in town and now I'm expected to do the same for the farmhouse at Elam.

Trouble is, there's no way our country Christmas tree will measure up to the city Christmas tree.

For one thing, the city Christmas tree was raised to be a Christmas tree on a Christmas tree farm, and whoever raised it did a good job.

It's perfect from any angle, with a straight trunk that fits into a Christmas tree stand and branches that are more or less evenly distributed from the base to the tip.

Christmas trees on the farm at Elam, on the other hand, are young cedars and pines that are currently growing where the birds and the wind planted them.

I start scouting for the best candidates among them just as soon as the weather cools off and I always find good ones.

*Holly for Christmas.*

The only trouble is, I can never find them again on Christmas eve which is the day we always cut and decorate the Elam tree.

The tree that looks perfect in the woods will lean at a twenty-degree angle in the living room.

Whole ranks of branches that were on the tree when I started cutting will have mysteriously vanished by the time the tree hits the ground.

The base of the tree will invariably be about an inch larger in diameter than the widest opening I can achieve on the Christmas tree stand.

Strings of Christmas tree lights that were carefully furled after last Christmas will have retangled themselves while stored away in boxes.

It's a frustrating chore, it always is, and I can't wait.

*December 1986*

We hear a lot of talk each year around this time about peace on earth, just about everybody's in favor of it.

But, sometimes it's easy to get the feeling that it's sorta like what Will Rogers said about the weather, that everybody talks about it but nobody does anything about it.

Well, maybe so, but tomorrow morning at seven, our time, which is twelve noon Greenwich time, an estimated four hundred million people will join hearts and thoughts around the globe on behalf of world peace.

The idea has been spreading for many months now and has been joined by people of more than seventy countries, representing all the world's religions and races and political systems.

And talk about grassroots. It's a program that has no organization, no funding, doesn't take up a collection, prescribes no particular form for sending a message to the Almighty, just a marvelous spreading of the word by people all over the world...

Alfred Lord Tennyson once wrote that "more things are wrought by prayer than this world dreams of"...

This moment of prayer for peace and harmony bears witness to that. Imagine, four hundred million people training their good will in the same direction at the same time...

All the mayors of Hampton Roads have proclaimed December 31 Worldwide Peace Prayer Day. More churches than I can name have joined in; there'll be gatherings and there will be individual prayers.

No rules, no dues, no signing up for a membership card. Just a bit of mental or spiritual energy directed toward peace and harmony on this planet.

At seven in the morning it will be the same day — New Year's eve — all over the world. But you don't have to wait until then — the lines are always open.

*December 1986*